A Layman Shares Jesus

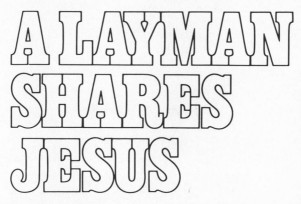

A LAYMAN SHARES JESUS

E. B. TOLES

1114 PARK BOULEVARD
ROME, GEORGIA 30161
USA

BROADMAN PRESS
Nashville, Tennessee

4255-06

ISBN: 0-8054-5506-X

Dewey Decimal Classification: 248.5

Subject heading: WITNESSING

Library of Congress Catalog Card Number: 78-67925

Printed in the United States of America

Foreword

This great book by E. B. Toles is one of the most inspiring testimonies to the goodness, mercy, and grace of an infinite and all-wise God that I have ever read. As a successful business-man and Georgia legislator who has served on many important committees in state government, he commands the respect and confidence of multiplied thousands of his fellow citizens of the state of Georgia, and the applause and appreciation of multitudes of fellow Christians not only in Georgia, but throughout the United States and across the world. He has also successfully served as an executive in the Georgia Baptist State Convention and has well represented his fellow Baptists.

From beginning to end, this book honors his Lord and glorifies his Savior. It proves beyond a shadow of any and all doubt to a thinking person that the sovereign God of the universe is more than vitally interested in every minute event of our lives. It also establishes the fact that God Almighty is still a magnificent and working God and able to use any and all circumstances and personalities who are totally dedicated to him and whose talents are readily available for the Master's use.

Obviously, here is one politician who has become an outstanding Christian statesman in his own political district and has been anointed of the Lord to tell the amazing story of what God has done in and through him. I highly recommend this book as a book of source material, for illustrations, for Sunday School teachers, ministers, and Christian workers, as well as a book of inspiration for any and all Christians who are excited about the high and holy privilege of serving a wonderful and risen Savior.

A *Layman Shares Jesus* will enrich your life and greatly strengthen your faith.

GRADY B. WILSON

Preface

This is a book from a unique layman. The author, E. B. Toles, has undergone many unusual spiritual and physical experiences.

The experiences recorded here were chosen to depict the long journey of a man who, at an early age, recognized that God was calling him to service, but who, for many years, sought to serve in his own way, on his own time schedule, rather than to follow God's will.

One of the most terrifying experiences in E. B.'s life—an experience which was to become a spiritual turning point—was an illness that altered his appearance for three years. It is rare for a person to suffer as many physical disabilities as E. B. and still be able to render an effective ministry.

E. B. has testified frequently: "Sometimes God leads his children through the fire, not that they might be destroyed but that they might be purified. This is true in my own life, as Job said, 'When he hath tried me, I shall come forth as gold.' "

God calls all of us to serve in some way—whether in our homes or "into all the world." As we grow in our walk with Jesus, we are often inclined to feel our Lord should be satisfied with us. But, as is dramatically shown here, God can allow crises to jolt us out of our peaceful self-content.

E. B. says, "I am simply a garden-variety Christian." And that helps us relate to him and his message.

E. B. has spent probably fifteen years in preparing this book. This is the testimony of a garden-variety Christian, successful businessman, and legislator, who has done the best he could to serve and magnify the Lord Jesus.

This book has been the object of much prayer from its inception. It was never anticipated that the book would be used to magnify any man, but to show through personal experiences and the eyes of others how God wins the life of an individual—and in turn uses that individual to win others.

A walk through these pages is, in many respects, like being

in the middle of a genuine revival. Every story recounted in these pages is true. Many personal experiences were not included because of space limitations.

In E. B.'s religious life, he has served in almost every position of responsibility in his home church, Second Avenue Baptist of Rome, Georgia. These positions have included Sunday School teacher, deacon, chairman of church committees, and adviser and counselor to people.

In denominational life, he has worked in successive and growing positions of responsibility. E. B. was elected first vice-president of the Georgia Baptist Convention in 1961 and served 1961–1962 in that position, as well as being a member of the Convention's executive committee.

In 1973 he was elected to a five-year term on the executive committee of the Georgia Baptist Convention. In 1975 he was made a member of the administration committee of the executive committee. In 1976 he was elected vice-chairman of that committee. He also served as a member of the Georgia Baptist Convention nominating committee in 1975, as well as a member of the Convention's committee on committees. Each state in the Southern Baptist Convention has one layman and one pastor to serve on the Convention's committee on boards. In 1976, at the annual Southern Baptist Convention, he was chosen to represent the state of Georgia as layman to serve on that committee.

Toles entered political life in 1968, when he was elected by a substantial majority to a seat in the Georgia General Assembly, where he has represented Rome and Floyd counties. He is widely recognized as a competent and responsible representative, as well as a Christian statesman.

In 1976 he was presented the "Christian Citizenship Citation" in appreciation for distinguished public service as a member of the General Assembly of Georgia, and for leadership efforts to strengthen Christian, ethical, and moral standards for the people and communities of Georgia. The citation was presented by the public affairs committee of the Georgia Baptist Convention. One of his most cherished experiences came in 1975, when the Georgia House of Representatives passed a resolution which recognized E. B. in a special way. Due to his deep and abiding religious faith and upon the receipt of a personal invitation from the President of the United States, Jimmy Carter, E. B. was chosen to represent the people of Georgia and the state House of Representatives at the National Prayer Breakfast in Washington, D.C.

He was a member of the Gideons International Association for many years and served as state chaplain of this organization for four years.

Today E. B. is in demand as a lay preacher for various churches, Bible conferences, and Christian businessmen's organizations across America.

JAMES A. LESTER

Contents

1

The Die Is Cast

It was a warm spring day in May. A boy of twelve was looking forward to the time when he could pull his shoes off and go barefoot. This is one of the things enjoyed by a boy in the country after the long, cold winter months. We counted the days from the almanac, waiting for the warm spring sunshine so we could rid ourselves of our shoes!

Our home had a fireplace in each room, but we were seldom allowed to build fires in the upstairs bedrooms. Before bedtime we warmed ourselves by the open fireplace in the parlor and then rushed upstairs to snuggle deep in our feather beds.

It was all very meaningful. It was real and precious because it was great to have, and be a part of, a large family and a Christian home.

Sunday was reserved solely as a day of worship and things our parents thought would be pleasing to the Lord. Anything of a "worldly" nature, such as pressing or mending clothes, was forbidden on Sunday; however, this was a happy time. Our family's relationship with the Lord was one of joy, characterized by a warmth of real love. One important part of Sunday was sharing this joy with others. We were rarely without guests for dinner, and the afternoons were spent visiting with friends and neighbors.

Bible reading and family prayer were important parts of our daily lives. Mother read and explained the Scriptures to us. It was her great desire that we would eventually make the decision to walk the way of the Lord throughout our lives and into eternity. There were seven children in our family, and all of us accepted Jesus Christ as Savior.

My dear mother was a great influence in my life. She was a woman of prayer, and her most ardent yearning was that God would use one of her children to preach the gospel.

My oldest sister says that Mother chose a place each day where she could be alone to pray. One of my sister's sweetest memories is seeing Mother as she left her place of prayer, wiping away the tears of joy, rejoicing, and singing praises to the Lord. Just by seeing her face, one would know she had been in touch with Jesus, whom she adored.

I learned things at my mother's knee that I never read from a textbook. She was a great Christian with a bedrock faith in God and lived to be eighty-four years old.

She would scold us and use the switch when we needed it, but the discipline she used most cut deep into the soul. First, she would sit down and talk with us in a sweet Christian spirit, using Scripture and prayer to show us the right way. The Holy Spirit would do the convicting, and it was much worse than a hard whipping. I would see tears in my precious mother's eyes when she knew we needed correcting. This type of discipline tore my heart out.

Lyerly, Georgia, was our home for many years, until one by one we left to seek our livelihood. Although it was a small community, boasting a population of about five hundred, its hills, creeks, river, and farms gave it a picturesque beauty. Farmers made up the majority of the population, but in those days the railroad had a tremendous influence on the growth of a town; and because Lyerly had a depot, there was incentive, opportunity, and need for merchants and businessmen.

Saturday was always a busy time in town. Farmers often brought their horses and mules to the blacksmith for shoeing. With awe we would watch the sparks fly from the anvil as the blacksmith beat and shaped the red-hot rod into horseshoes.

No matter what business brought the families to town, as train time neared, all ears were tuned for the engine's shrill whistle. As the train approached the refueling station outside of town, young and old alike found it exciting and breathtaking to watch the train round the bend and slowly approach the depot. We never tired of speculating about the lives of the travelers and their destinations.

After the train had been unloaded and continued on its way, the youngsters gathered at the drugstore to sip Cokes and sodas. The older men sat on the boardwalk, passing the time of day, chewing tobacco, discussing politics, religion, farming, and the weather, while waiting for the postmaster to sort the newly arrived mail.

It was the first Sunday in August, and as usual the protracted meeting at the Lyerly Baptist Church was being held. My twin sister made the decision to ask Jesus Christ to come into her heart, and she was saved.

Seeing the joy and fulfillment this brought to her, that night at my mother's knee I, too, accepted Christ as Lord and Savior of my life. We all rejoiced. I could hardly wait for the next night's service, to make my profession of faith known to the church and to all others who knew me, and to begin living a Christian life.

Although my concept of sin was rather well developed at an early age, it was not until I accepted the Lord Jesus that the devil began to work on me so that I was aware of him, placing temptation and stumbling blocks in my path. As every Christian knows, Satan never lets up; but it is because of this that we gain a deeper understanding of what being saved and being born again really mean.

A couple of weeks after my conversion, Mother gave me permission to wear my first long pants and treasured Ingersoll dollar pocket watch. This was a dream come true and a great event!

While playing on the bank of the creek near home, one of my playmates pushed me into the creek. Fearing my watch and pants were ruined, in an angry moment I called him a "little devil." This word, so hastily spoken, I considered among the worst of profanities; and it gave me my first searing burden of sin.

My conscience began to hurt. Quickly I ran home and told Mother what had happened, and then in shame I revealed to her the words I had called my playmate. "Mother, I have sinned. Will God forgive me for using such language?"

Mother, always patient and understanding, gently took me upstairs to my bedroom and read 1 Corinthians 10:13: "There hath no temptation taken you but such as is common to man: but God is faithful, who will not suffer you to be tempted above that ye are able; but will with the temptation also make a way to escape, that ye may be able to bear it." On her knees she asked God to forgive me. Then I prayed, "Please, dear Lord Jesus, forgive me for using such bad words; and I'll never do it again." I felt the burden of guilt lifted from me.

Those few moments with Mother, the prayers and Scripture engraved on my heart, have been a blessing through the years. I can truthfully say I have never taken God's name in vain. My mother's words and teachings were deeply embedded in my heart. They have caused me always to watch my language. When something goes wrong and temptation comes, my thoughts and memories return immediately to the upstairs bedroom prayer and creek bank experience and that verse, 1 Corinthians 10:13. It became a soothing balm that helped to heal during developments in my life which brought me grief, sorrow, heartache, and physical and mental pain.

Perhaps many of you have not had the joy and experience of being reared in a Christian home as I have. Let me assure you, we must each meet the temptations and crossroads of life; and God allows us the freedom of choice.

References to my mother are frequent because of the impact she had upon my life. We had a neighbor who had a beautiful flower garden. One day friends came to visit our family, and all of them went to view her flowers. One of the friends stepped on the flowers, and the neighbor became very upset. Mother would never knowingly cause discord among friends or neighbors. Together we went to our neighbor's home. While walking, Mother reminded me that Jesus uses every opportunity to do good and to prove his love.

Upon arrival Mother said, "I have come to apologize for the damage accidentally done to your flower garden. I love you and trust you will accept my apology. Here's a cake I baked for you, and I feel this will express my sincere feelings toward you as my neighbor."

I saw love between neighbors and the meaning of forgiveness. I saw the Scripture "Thou shalt love thy neighbor as thyself" (Matt. 19:19) in action. Someone had to take the first step, and my mother chose to do so. This lesson of Christian love has stayed with me. Mother was a devout Christian who used Jesus' teachings as a way of life to be practiced. It was important to her that we experience the meaning of Christian love.

Although I did not realize it at the time, these numerous, seemingly insignificant, daily occurrences in my early life were bringing me to a closer walk with the Lord. These were all God-ordained preparations for the long journey ahead. Sometimes I stumbled and lost my way in darkness, but I returned to the path chosen at my mother's knee.

My parents were frugal. We children had many homemade gifts and very few "store-bought" toys. My sister and I were so eager to purchase a bicycle that we asked the principal of the high school, which was across the street from our home, if he would give us the job of building fires in the potbellied stove each morning so we could earn enough money to buy a bicycle. We were paid ten dollars per month. This was a great learning experience for us.

In 1929 the Great Depression was upon us. My father was concerned during these trying days. On one occasion Mother knew he was troubled, and she said, "Let's don't worry about these problems; let's pray and believe that God will see us through." We had plenty to eat and plenty of clothes. We had many things for which to be thankful. Father owned farms and had sharecroppers and tenants. He was a successful farmer and merchant, well known throughout Chatooga County and nearby Georgia and Alabama towns. He served on the school board and was mayor of Lyerly for several years. He believed his children should have responsibility and learn how to work. Rain or shine, he had a job waiting for us. He would not tolerate idleness. His motto was, "An idle mind is the devil's workshop."

After finishing high school, I wanted to earn my own money. I applied for a job in the drugstore at Lyerly. The pharmacist offered to pay me a dollar a day. The first Saturday I worked, he wanted to see how much "stickability" I had, so he put me in the back of the drugstore, bottling castor oil. In my childhood we knew of only two types of medicine: castor oil and calomel. The druggist would buy the castor oil in five-gallon drums or wooden kegs, from which it was dispensed into fifteen-, twenty-, and twenty-five-cent bottles. That first day the odor of the oil made me sick, but I stayed with the job. The next Saturday it was my job to bottle castor oil again. I returned, determined, and told him I could handle it. By holding my nose and gritting my teeth, I turned the handle, drew the castor oil, bottled it, and labeled it. I made it through the second Saturday; and when the pharmacist realized that I would stick with the work, he gave me a regular job and did not make me handle the castor oil keg again.

I had a keen yearning in my heart for Jesus, and I desired to live a Christian life; but as most boys do when they get older, I wanted to enjoy the "pleasures" of life. Because I was a Christian, these "pleasures" never really made me happy; nor did I have peace in my heart. The problem was "overrated pleasures," "underrated treasures." Regretfully, I failed God in many ways as a young man.

An answer to prayer finally ended this detour I had taken from God's path. Often I had prayed that God would give me a Christian wife, one whom I could respect, honor, and love with all my heart. Mildred and I were married soon after the depression. My life changed completely, and until this day she remains everything I asked for and more. We rejoice in the blessings God has bestowed upon us.

During the years immediately following the Great Depression, jobs were scarce and one would be fortunate indeed to find work paying twenty-five dollars a week. After a brief employment with an insurance company, I went to work as a salesman for a local furniture store. One of my brothers worked for the same furniture store, and the other brother became manager of the furniture department in the largest chain store in America. The three of us agreed to learn all the business principles necessary, so that eventually we could go into business for ourselves. This was the goal we worked toward, one which would not be realized for several years.

God had plans for my life and tried to reveal them to me in the early years of my marriage. Often these were years of one-way communication. I would pray, but I would not listen. It seemed every day God was trying to reach me, and the pressure kept getting worse day by day. I was hesitant about discussing this difficult problem with anyone. I thought that contributing financially to churches, ministers, evangelists, and anyone else who had a need would please God. I leaned heavily upon this crutch, but it did not satisfy the longing and tugging in my soul.

After World War II our country was struggling to return to normal—the soldiers were coming home and merchants were receiving many items that we had been deprived of during the war years. There was exhilaration and hope everywhere that our country would make a speedy recovery. Merchandising was in for a new day.

My brothers and I decided that now was the time to venture into business. We opened a furniture store, and with long hours and hard work we soon began to prosper. Our business grew by leaps and bounds, and God came first. We operated according to Christian principles. Soon we had ten employees working with us, selling furniture. One of our rules was never to employ a person without telling him we would not tolerate profanity or irreverent language, and we operated on Christian principles regardless of possible gain. Prosperity, however, was not the answer to my troubled soul—God was speaking to me. He wanted me to work for him, to speak his Word. Many times I would leave the store, go out to the mountains, and lift my heart to God in prayer.

People would come into the store and say, "Toles, you should be a preacher." I was ever conscious of these almost unbearable words; and oh, how they cut into my heart and soul! God

wanted me to give my life to him and get on with his work,
but I rebelled and refused to let him have his way with my
life. I was too attached to material things: money and business.
God was good to us, and we were now financially able to
build our first home. Building the bungalow was a happy event
in our lives. Mildred loves flowers, and soon she had one of
the prettiest yards on the street. Owning a thriving business
and a new home naturally played a part in keeping me from
surrendering my life completely to the will of God. I was a
miserable wretch and sick in body every day.

Working for years under this stress and strain is beyond de-
scription. I became despondent and even thought that to end
my life would be the best way out. I wonder now how I sur-
vived, but God was in it all. He was working out his plan for
my life.

My mother, with her wisdom and complete faith and trust
in God, knew the day of surrender would come; but she never
did tell me I must preach. She wanted *God* to do the calling.

One day a strange thing happened as I went into the post
office. There was a large picture of "Uncle Sam," with his finger
pointing straight toward me, saying, "I Want You." Those words
rang in my ears as God spoke to me and said, "I want you,
son, I want you." The words came forth from my lips before
I realized what I was saying: "Oh, no! No! Not me, God, not
me!" I never got away from those words and thoughts.

I had a complete physical change. Practically overnight all
my thick, black, wavy hair came out. I went three years in
this condition, with no whiskers, eyebrows, eyelashes, or hair
on my head. I never placed a razor on my face! Many of my
friends did not recognize me, and this in itself was almost
enough to drive a person insane. Thank God I made it through!
I am sure I quoted one of my favorite verses of Scripture over
a thousand times during these dark days: "Call unto me, and
I will answer thee, and shew thee great and mighty things,
which thou knowest not" (Jer. 33:3).

Finally, after visiting several medical doctors and specialists,
I was advised to see a psychiatrist. This I resented. I knew I

was not mentally ill but only very foolish and not willing to
come out with the real problem that had been bottled up inside
me for years. Now I had reached the crossroad in my life—it
was life or death.

I finally went to the psychiatrist. He said, "Tell it all." But
I would not tell it all. I could not tell him the truth. However,
on the fourth trip he wisely said, "You're lying, and it might
cost you your life."

I *was* lying, and I knew it. How foolish can a man be! I
knew I was lying, and yet I was paying the doctor a large
sum to tell me what I already knew. At last I saw the light,
but still I resisted surrender. I am convinced it took this psychiatrist to make me realize death was near; eternity and judgment
were facing me.

One who has never had the "shingles" (Herpes Zoster—a
cluster of blisters on the body) cannot fathom what agonizing
and excruciating pain and suffering the infection causes. The
pain is so bad that you want to tear the skin from your body!
In a measure I know something of what Job meant: "And he
took him a potsherd to scrape himself withal; and he sat down
among the ashes" (Job 2:8).

During the weeks of this dreadful illness that plagued my
body, it was necessary to stay in my bedroom without a stitch
of clothing on—I could not stand the touch of cloth to the
skin. Many times I prayed to God the words of Job, "Oh, that
I might have my request: and that God would grant me the
thing that I long for!" (Job 6:8).

So much illness during the early years of my married life
made me realize that, at best, life is short. I had a deep feeling
I would not live very long, for my physical condition grew
steadily worse. I read the Bible daily and would search out a
quiet place for prayer and meditation. I would wait for God
to speak peace to my soul, but the peace never came. I spent
a small fortune in and out of hospitals, seeking health—Mayo
Clinic, Duke Hospital, specialists, and some of the best doctors
in America. I was only skin and bone. They tried everything
in the book, from drinking goat's milk to breathing in a paper

bag every hour of the day. Heart, brain, spinal, X rays, clinical examinations—you name it; there was not a physical test that I did not try. Not only was I sick physically, but I was also sick spiritually. God in his divine wisdom knew how and where to break my stubborn will. It was a health problem that God permitted before I finally surrendered.

I was much like Jonah. Jonah's fate was really a blessing in disguise. He was not worth the salt in his bread for God until the big fish came along and swallowed him. This was true in my life. Sometimes God will speak to us by putting a whale in our lives. Perhaps there is a certain amount of Jonah in all of us. After all, who has not, on occasions, been a Jonah and refused to obey a clear call from the Lord? The entire book of Jonah contains only forty-eight verses, but the words are packed with a wealth of spiritual truths that will teach us much if we are only willing to take heed.

We must learn that God never makes a mistake, regardless of what comes our way in life. Truly, life's hardships are intended to make us better, not bitter.

2
Turning Point

It is strange how God prepares everything down to the right second, the precise place, and the exact words to be spoken.

One day my brothers and I were in the office, discussing future plans for our business. Aware of the struggle in my life, one of them said, "Eventually you are going to have to *preach.*" It was like a bolt of lightning, a dagger to my heart. Although the Lord had tried to reveal his plan many times, it was the word "preach" that did it. At that moment I realized that this was God's plan for my life.

For a moment I was silent; then with tears in my eyes, stunned, I took their hands and said, "This is it! This is it! This is it! O God, forgive me! O God, this is it!"

They asked me to calm down and explain what I meant by, "This is it!" I felt as if I could fly. The burden was lifted! I could not explain to them the joy and peace that flooded my soul. The burden rolled away. The thing which I knew would happen one day came unexpectedly, and I was unprepared. But God knows the hour, the moment, the second, the words to break a stubborn will. I felt a great burden lifted from my body and soul. Words are inadequate to explain the release, the peace, the joy, and the happiness that engulfed me when I finally heard God's call. I knew it was the call of God because the burden was gone.

I immediately went home and fell on my knees, asking God's forgiveness. Then opening my Bible at random, I glued my eyes to the Scripture, "Therefore to him that knoweth to do good, and doeth it not, to him it is sin" (Jas. 4:17).

I said, "O Lord, I know what you want me to do, and I'm

going to do it if it kills me . . . Lord, this is it." I meant business
with God that day, come what may. Business, home, success—
I surrendered all. For years I had known and feared that total
surrender to God might mean giving up my home and business.
How would my wife accept this? Those fears were so exagger-
ated and became as nothing!

My wife joined me in fervent prayer. I told her everything
that had been locked up in my soul for years relative to God's
call in my life. This was the very first night of rest for soul
and body that I had had in years. The psalmist said, "Commit
thy way unto the Lord; trust also in him; and he shall bring
it to pass" (Ps. 37:5).

The following Sunday at church, when my pastor gave the
invitation, I immediately went forward and told him of my
decision. Then, turning to the congregation, I told them what
God had done. I asked the organist to play my favorite hymn,
"Take Your Burden to the Lord and Leave It There." How
great it was, standing there singing and praising God with that
tremendous joy and unbounded happiness! The congregation
joined me in rejoicing and praising God.

The next week things began to happen: God was leading,
and it was a beautiful picture to see how he was controlling
my life moment by moment, day by day. The pastor of a small
church, whom I had known for many years, came to our store
and said, "I want you to come preach in my church next Sunday." He was not aware of what had taken place in my life.
"Isn't this strange!" he said. "God told me to come to you."
God was unveiling his plan.

I recall saying to my wife, "God is in this, and something
good is going to come from this."

The sermon I prepared was simple. God impressed it on
my heart to speak of blind Bartimaeus, recorded in Mark 10:46–
52. Three souls were saved that night, and for me that was
God's stamp of approval. In my mind there was no doubt—I
must move forward with God. There was no turning back now;
it was a forward march!

I believe what the Bible says in Romans 8:28: "And we know

that all things work together for good to them that love God, to them who are the called according to his purpose." Although we may never understand in this life, there is no doubt in my mind that God has a purpose and reason for everything that happens in a Christian's life.

Then the first trial came: The devil tried to turn me back and make me renounce God. One morning, the following week, I awoke at 5 A.M. with one of the horrible migraine headaches that had troubled me for years. I was in such terrible pain that I could not lift my head from the pillow. During the many years before my surrender, the pain of these headaches had been so severe that doctors would give me shots to sedate me.

On this occasion Satan would have had me think God had forsaken me. Painfully and hardly able to speak, I said, "Get thee behind me, Satan!" I asked my wife to call my mother and my sister; and when they arrived, I said, "Mother, I want all three of you to get on your knees around this bed. God is going to perform a miracle this morning. There is no doubt in my mind." God had spoken to my soul; I cannot explain it, but I knew it!

Mother, with all her wisdom, said, "Son, are you sure you know what you are saying?" She was not doubting God's power to heal my body, but she wanted to make sure I knew what I was asking of God, to call upon him in such an hour. They read the verses I asked for and prayed on their knees. Then I prayed a simple, short prayer. "O God, remove this terrible condition from my body, this migraine headache. Please, dear Lord. I'm your child and I have surrendered all to your will. Now, Lord, your servant lays claim to your promise and all honor, glory, and praise I give to Thee; hear me, dear Lord!" Immediately God wiped away that terrible headache and quieted my entire body. That was twenty-five years ago, and not once since that morning have I had a migraine headache!

This definite answer to a prayer was a great victory for me. It taught me something I had never experienced before—I had felt the touch of the Master's hand. This made me well aware that money and success in business were not the answers; neither did they satisfy. God had something better for me. Life is full of distress and problems. Jesus Christ never promised to remove all the problems of life, but he did promise to give us the grace that we need to keep us going. He is the shelter in the time of storm. He gives us strength in the midst of all our problems.

For the next few months, many hours were spent on my knees in prayer and Bible study and in memorizing the Scriptures. The Word of God became alive and real and a blessing to my life.

With the advice of many of my preacher-friends, I began to acquire as many Bible commentaries as I could. I read and studied the lives of great preachers: biographies of Dwight L. Moody, Charles H. Spurgeon, John Wesley, George W. Truett, and many others, including many contemporary "giants of God." These and other biographies of men of God fill the shelves in my study today. After studying their lives, I summarized all of their success in four words: prayer, Bible study, and obedience. Although these books with their Bible helps are good, no book will take the place of the Holy Bible!

Through experience I have learned that the more devout a person is, the more he values the Word of God. The man who rarely samples the Word of God does not develop a taste for it. "O taste and see that the Lord is good: blessed is the man that trusteth in him" (Ps. 34:8). A holy life would not be so rare or so difficult if our devotions were not so short and hurried.

We live shabbily because we pray shortly. J. Wilbur Chapman said, "The rule that governs my life . . . anything that dims my vision of Christ or takes away my taste for Bible study or cramps my prayer life or makes Christian work difficult . . . is wrong for me . . . and I must turn away from it."

No man can tell how rich he is by thumbing through his ledgers. He is rich according to what he *is*, not what he *has*. God does not measure a man by his pocketbook or a tape measure around his head, but one around his heart. It is the heart that makes a man rich.

I shall never forget what one of my dear old preacher-friends once said to me, "If you want power with God, son, you get just as far as you possibly can from the world."

Daniel Webster once was asked, "Sir, what is the most important question ever to enter your mind?" Webster replied, "My individual responsibility to my God." Day by day I became more aware of my own individual responsibility to my God.

My mother gave me a gospel tract over twenty years ago, and I keep it in my billfold. Its words have been a guiding light to me. In brief, it says, "God wants you to have something far better than gold: a helpless dependency on him that he may have the privilege of supplying your need day by day out of an unseen measure. He will make you work without knowing how much you are doing. The Holy Spirit will put a strict watch over you with a jealous love. He may not explain a thousand things which puzzle your reason in his dealing with you, but he says, 'My grace is sufficient for thee: for my strength is made perfect in weakness' (2 Cor. 12:9). 'Set your affections on things above, not on things on the earth. For ye are dead, and your life is hid with Christ in God' (Col. 3:2-3).

"If God has called you to be really like Jesus, he will draw you into a life of crucifixion and humility. He may let others be great and you small. He may let others get the credit for the work you have done, making your reward ten times greater when Jesus comes."

Day by day I was overwhelmed by the descent of the Holy Spirit upon me. It seemed that the impression was like a wave of electricity, the very breath of Almighty God. His wonderful love was shed abroad in my heart; and it was real because it was God.

He had a plan and purpose for my life, but I did not want to go his way; I wanted to go my way. "There is a way that seemeth right unto a man, but the end thereof are the ways of death" (Prov. 16:25).

Thank God, he spared me to live through it all. As the song says: "Through it all, I've learned to trust in Jesus, I've learned to trust in God." Truly God knows the way to break the rebellious will of a stubborn man. The marvelous mercy of God was made clear in my life. I am sure I questioned God a thousand times before complete surrender. Why me, O God? Why these terrible migraine headaches? Why must my physical body suffer so much anguish, pain, and sickness?

I confess I sinned many times when I would see others with healthy, strong bodies. I would envy them and ask, "Why? Why?" It became as clear as the pure spring water that flows from the mountain: It was simply God's way in my life.

Like so many other Christians, I had been wading around in shallow water far too long; and it was now time for me to launch out into the deep for my wonderful Lord, leaving the physical problems with God, trusting him.

The apostle Paul had a thorn in the flesh (2 Cor. 12:7-10). Three times he sought the Lord about this problem, and he learned that the infirmities and distress were necessary because they made him strong in the Lord. Hebrews 12:6 tells us, "For whom the Lord loveth he chasteneth." This one thing I know, *God surely loves me!* Few people really know the chastisement I have had in my life: in and out of hospitals innumerable times. There is no doubt in my mind that if I had not surrendered my life to God's will, I would be in the cemetery today.

3
God's Timetable

It was evident that I needed to be better prepared for the Lord's work. There were several years of sorrow and sad experience as I searched out preachers and laymen, seeking help and advice. I thought the knowledge of these men could show the way. The Scripture says: "This is the way, walk ye in it" (Isa. 30:21).

Looking back, I realize that God's plan was perfect, and it was a part of God's timetable that I should receive an invitation to a Bible conference at Lake Louise (now the Georgia Baptist Assembly) in Toccoa, Georgia. My wife and I decided to accept the invitation.

After the first service my attention was drawn to an elderly man. Knowing that this man, Dr. Charles F. Weigle, was on the program, we introduced ourselves. After talking awhile, he invited us to his room. I am sure the Spirit of the Lord revealed to him that I was searching for God's direction. Some years later he revealed to me that God had spoken to him about my problem.

Dr. Weigle was eighty-two years old and on the staff at Tennessee Temple College in Chattanooga, Tennessee. During our frequent visits he would often tell of his experiences with men of God such as Billy Sunday and others of his day. Not only was Dr. Weigle a great preacher and evangelist, but he was also a great songwriter. One of his best-known songs is "No One Ever Cared for Me Like Jesus."

I had a tremendous desire to become better acquainted with this man of God, so on our way home from Toccoa, we stopped in Chattanooga and visited again with Dr. Weigle. He intro-

duced me to Dr. Lee Roberson, a dedicated servant of the
Lord, president and founder of the Tennessee Temple College,
and pastor of the Highland Park Baptist Church in Chattanooga. I shall always be grateful to Dr. Roberson for the interest
and the help he gave me. How marvelous and mysterious are
God's ways! Although I was unaware at the time, another prayer
was being answered.

After talking to Dr. Roberson and seeing the college in ses-
sion, I was greatly impressed and felt the Holy Spirit had
brought me to that great man of God and the college for a
purpose. There was a positive feeling that Temple was where
God wanted me to get the preparation to do his work.

Upon returning home, my wife and I discussed the matter
and prayed about it. Because of my age I knew studying and
memorizing Scriptures would be difficult, but God had called
me; and I put everything in his care. The next semester I
enrolled in Temple College with the blessings of my two brothers and partners in business. They were good to me, and I
shall always be grateful to them.

I left my business and closed our newly built home. My wife
and I moved into a three-room, upstairs apartment near the
college. The abrupt change from our routine life and our tidy
home to uncertainty, disorder, cramped quarters, and the un-
pleasant job of evicting some insects made me ponder, "O
my Lord, what have I gotten into now?" My wife, a brave
and stalwart Christian, stuck by me. She said, "Let's stick it
out; God will take care of us."

My health was improving, and many good things were happening. Just think how close I had come to missing the great
blessings and the great privileges that I have had in this life
for the last thirty-five years!

The fulfillment of my preparation was not complete until I
took all the courses available in Bible school, college, and semi-
nary. No plans were made beyond this because I still did not
know how God would use me. I had faith that he would open
the doors and use me. God had blessed me while I was attend-

ing school. After completing my education, I returned to Rome and our furniture business.

We can never know the perpetual ministry of one little tract. We experienced this many times from the tracts given and taken from the tract box attached to the front door of our furniture store. It was our custom to encourage all who entered the door to take one or more tracts with them, and every order was delivered with a tract enclosed. This was one way we could send the message of God's love to others.

Here is one interesting example. In October of 1971, a letter came from one of our customers ten years after the man left town. The letter in its entirety follows:

"I moved off years ago from Rome. I owe you Toles boys $129. *Please divide this.* God makes me do this. P.S. He is not dead." The postal money order was enclosed.

There were many interesting experiences and discussions about the Lord's business. I have tried to keep a record of individuals who came to know Christ as Lord and Savior through the tracts and testimonies during business hours. It would be impossible to have a complete record. Only God knows the distance one little tract may have traveled and how many hearts and lives might have accepted the Lord Jesus. The seed was planted, and only God knows how great the harvest; but someday, some glorious day, I will meet them in heaven. And to God we give all the praise and all the glory.

I thank God for each opportunity that has been mine in speaking to others about the Lord Jesus.

"But as we were allowed of God to be put in trust with the gospel, even so we speak; not as pleasing men, but God, which trieth our hearts" (1 Thess. 2:4).

Soul-winning is every Christian's job, not just the preacher's. One must be willing to let God lead and use him. The will of God will never be done in a man's life unless the Spirit within him is stirred to do so.

I remember one of my good friends, a deacon, who used to trade with me. On many occasions when he came into my store to pay on his account, we would sit and talk. I always looked forward to seeing him. He made a statement that I have always remembered: "If yo' religion ain't changed you—you better change yo' religion." I had to say a big "Amen" to that.

One of the best concepts in biblical theology he taught me came when I went to the local hospital where he worked, to visit a sick friend. We happened to meet in the corridor and stopped to chat. The conversation soon centered around the subject of holy living. We discussed the fact that far too many church members never really get to the place where they are willing to live a holy life.

He said, "Mr. Toles, let me tell you something. You know on de front of de Bible it say Holy Bible, don't it?"

I replied quickly, "Yes, generally that is true on the cover of most Bibles."

"Well," he said, "you turn that Bible over. On de back side of it, it don't say nuthing, do it?" I said, "That's right." "Well, dat's de way it is with you—you is either holy or you ain't nothing."

I walked away, saying, "Thank God for a man who can think such thoughts." Even though he was not well educated, he knew the Lord and was wise. He knew about holy living.

Charles H. Spurgeon once said, "The world is full of counterfeits, our own hearts are deceitful, so that truth lies not on the surface, but must be drawn up from the deepest well. We must search ourselves very anxiously and very thoroughly. We are, in a certain sense, our own tools, and therefore, must keep ourselves in order. Every workman knows the necessity of keeping his tools in a good state of repair."

It is said that Michelangelo understood so well the importance of his tools that he always made his own brushes. In this he gives us an illustration of the grace of God, who with special care fashions for himself all true disciples.

It is human nature to resist sacrifices; yet it is a fact of life that carrying the accumulations of the past makes a slow walk toward a better future. We must forget our childish ways to obtain adulthood. In the business world there have to be sacrifices for success, and in the Christian life there is a sacrifice day by day. The more we cling to earthly treasures, the less room there is for God's blessings in our lives. Many are not willing to pay the price, but we must never forget the words of the apostle Paul in writing to the Philippians: "Let this mind be in you, which was also in Christ Jesus: Who, being in the form of God, thought it not robbery to be equal with God: But made himself of no reputation, and took upon him the form of a servant, and was made in the likeness of men: And being found in fashion as a man, he humbled himself, and became obedient unto death, even the death of the cross" (Phil. 2:5-8).

Keep in mind that nothing is impossible with God. He eagerly awaits our decisions to be used as tools in his service. Let me remind you that we are all just tools in God's garden: some spades—some rakes—some hoes—some diggers. But each has its place and serves a purpose, if used. Let us prove that we are his servants by our actions.

It is recorded that the great French artist Monet once said, "There are three kinds of people: (1) those who don't know what's happening; (2) those who don't care what's happening; (3) those who make things happen." It is my desire to be numbered among those who make things happen.

I am reminded of the words of my good deacon-friend, "Mr. Toles, you know your religion is much like building a fire, but you got to keep throwing kindling on the fire to stay warm." "Oh," I said, "words to remember." The older I get, the more I realize we must keep the fire burning in our hearts and souls.

My daily prayer is, "Lord, help me to keep the fire burning in my heart and soul. Help me to let my light shine so others may truly know I have been with Jesus."

Buttercup Experience

Perhaps to invite you along on a recent trip would best explain the following experience. Having a desire to go back to some of the old places I had known during my early childhood,

I drove out on a lonely dirt road in the country. There was no noise of the city. I was away from it all. It was early March, and one could hear the wind whistling through the branches of the large oak trees. I noticed that the old barn was weather-beaten and that the sheet-metal roof was loose and moved with each breeze. The weatherboard siding had rotted away, and there were big holes in many places. Looking across the road, I saw a brick and rock chimney where once stood a lovely, comfortable country home that had burned to the ground. All the people had long since left this old plantation. No one was around for miles. The quietness was comfortable and relaxing. I could not resist the urge to get out and walk around and reminisce, comparing life to the beauty and wonders of God and nature. It seemed as if I had relived my whole life, realizing that someday I, too, would fade away, but the world would continue. (While here, however, I have a job to do.)

Suddenly I was thrilled, and a feeling of joy and happiness overwhelmed me, as my eyes were fixed on a beautiful array of little yellow buttercups that had just bloomed. Oh, how beautiful was that place! I began to think. The buttercups did not care whether the president would be reelected or what party would elect the winner that year; neither did they have any anxiety for the future. Rather, they just did their job, which was to be beautiful and bountiful. They came by the command of God and at his desire. They had no gardener or caretaker. Nevertheless, they did their job, showing to the world all their beauty and glorification of God.

The little buttercups are the first to show their beauty. Regardless of how cold and dreary it may be, they still come forth because God knows and cares. If we could just learn the simple lesson of the buttercups and do our job and be faithful stewards year-in, year-out, what a different world it would be!

4

No Way Out

Upon arriving home after a long day at our store, I was called by a friend, who said, "This afternoon I have been talking with a man who is in desperate trouble. I need your help. Will you come now and go with me to his place of business?" I left immediately.

When we reached his place of business, the man was pacing the floor. It was obvious that he was desperate and in dire need of help. Wringing his hands, he kept repeating, "There is no way out, no way out."

I tapped him on the shoulder and said, "Now, my dear friend, wait a minute. There *is* a way out." He paused for a moment and looked at me inquisitively as I began reading from my Testament: "Jesus saith unto him, I am the way, the truth, and the life: no man cometh unto the Father but by me" (John 14:6). I handed him the Bible and said, "Now read it out loud."

He read it and said, "Jesus saith, I am the way." This is as far as the man could read.

He repeated it and I asked, "What does it say?"

He replied, "Jesus saith, I am the way." I could see it was becoming meaningful to him.

I put my arm around him. "Do you believe these words?"

He thought for a moment and said, "I don't know if I do or not. I am not sure I know what I believe."

I said, "I don't know what your problem is, but there is a way out, and it is only through Jesus Christ. He is the mediator between God and man."

I could feel the Holy Spirit at work. The man stood as though frozen in his tracks. I kept quoting simple Scriptures. "Sir, you are a desperate man and you need help."

"I surely do."

"I'll tell you what let's do. Walk to the front door, lock it, and put out the lights. Will you do it right now?" By now, the Holy Spirit had revealed to me that this man needed to know of the power of God.

He thought for a moment and moved toward the front door and locked it. As he came back to where I was standing, he pulled the cord on each light fixture that was hanging from the ceiling.

I said, "Now, come with me." We walked to the rear of his store and sat down. I began to read the Bible to him.

He said, "I'm afraid it's too late." Then we read John 6:37: "[Jesus said], him that cometh to me, I will in no wise cast out."

"Are you willing to call upon God, to ask God to help you?"

He thought for a moment and finally said, "Yes, I am." We went to our knees in prayer. I began to pour out my heart for him, still not knowing his problem.

Tears began to flow down his cheeks, and I turned my Bible to Romans 10:9-10 and said, "Now, I want you to listen to this. The Bible says "That if thou shalt confess with thy mouth [believe in his heart, not his head but his heart] . . . , thou shalt be saved." I explained how he could confess and believe from the heart. Jesus revealed himself to that man in an unusual way. As a matter of fact, I witnessed an experience there that I had never seen before: the light of the Lord Jesus made its way into his heart. He realized that Jesus was the way.

He got up and said, "Thank you, Lord. Thank you, God, for saving me!" He invited me back into his office at the front of the building.

As we sat at his desk, he reached into the drawer, pulled out a .32 caliber revolver, and laid it on top of his desk. "Mr. Toles, you can have that."

"I don't need that gun, sir," I replied.

Again he opened a desk drawer, pulled out several insurance policies, and tore them up. With tears in his eyes, he said,

"Mr. Toles, if you had not come tonight, I had planned to take my life because I thought there was no other way. But, thank God, I have found Jesus; and I am going home and tell my wife what has happened."

That man became a great Christian in his church. I watched his life for several years after that. I learned from the experience that you never know whether a visit might be a life-or-death matter to the person to whom you are witnessing.

Some weeks later the man called me. "I've read something in the Bible that is so precious to me. Let me read it to you."

I listened as he read from his Bible, "Am I a God at hand, saith the Lord, and not a God afar off? Can any hide himself in secret places that I shall not see him? saith the Lord. Do not I fill heaven and earth? saith the Lord" (Jer. 23:23-24).

"Mr. _____, go on with God; there are many great things in store for you. Keep praying, reading your Bible, and letting others know what Jesus Christ has done for you. This makes life worth living."

A big "Amen" came in reply.

God's Miraculous Ways

Early one morning, while I was shaving, I was silently reviewing the busy schedule that lay ahead. God kept penetrating my thoughts until, in spite of all my appointments and business obligations, there seemed to be an overwhelming desire to win someone to Christ that day. I yielded my thoughts to the Lord and uttered a prayer: "Dear Lord, lead me to some soul today who is searching for you, or send someone my way that I might tell what Christ means to me." Before breakfast I shared this desire with my wife, and together we prayed for God to use me in a special way.

The day proceeded in the usual way, except for my prayerful expectation of the Lord's work. About midmorning I was standing near the front entrance of our store as a young man walked in and said, "Sir, I am in a financial bind and have some other problems that necessitate selling my furniture. Would you be interested in buying what I have?"

As he talked, I reached into the tract box by the door, pulled out a gospel tract, and placed it in his hand. Almost immediately I felt the Holy Spirit speaking to me: "Here is the answer to your prayer."

To answer his question, I said, "Come over here where we can sit down. If you want to tell me the nature of your problem, perhaps there might be a way for me to help."

He had just been released from the state tuberculosis hospital after spending two years for cure of the illness. His wife had moved to Rome from South Georgia to be near him; and now they wanted to return home, but they were without money.

After a few minutes of conversation, I asked if he were a Christian. He responded in a surprised tone of voice, "Why did you ask me that?" I shared with him my love for Christ and my desire that everyone should know our beloved Savior. Realizing we could not talk openly in the midst of the busy activity within the store, I invited him to a secluded alcove in the warehouse, that was often used as a place of prayer.

He related his past: He was a Korean War veteran, brought up in a small country town where his father was a preacher. Tears came to his eyes as he spoke of the times his father had urged him to accept Christ into his life. When he became of age, he entered the service without making his decision for Christ. His father passed away before he was discharged from the military. Since then his mother also had passed away.

There was no doubt in my mind that God had sent that man to me. We read some Scriptures, and he earnestly expressed his desire to be saved. We prayed about his burdens and he asked Christ into his life. As we rejoiced together and praised God, he said, "Mr. Toles, very early this morning I got on my knees and asked God to send me to someone who would help. I rode the bus downtown, passing three furniture stores; but I made no effort to leave the bus before reaching your corner." My heart leaped for joy as I told how I, too, had prayed for God to send someone my way.

"It's a miracle!" he exclaimed.

"Yes, God's wonders never cease!"

"Oh, if only my parents could know of my decision," he said.

"They do, my friend. God answered the prayers of your parents, and now they and all of heaven are rejoicing with us."

We went to his apartment and told his wife what had happened. I spoke to her about accepting Christ, and she joyfully asked him into her life and was gloriously saved. Then I gave them the amount needed for returning to their home in South Georgia. We parted, rejoicing in the miraculous power of God and how he had brought us together. That is among my most treasured experiences in service to God. When he answers prayer, the result is often much more than we ask. To sow the seed is true happiness, but to know that the seed has ripened for harvest is a divine blessing to the heart and soul.

About two years later a healthy, well-dressed man approached me as I was working in the office. With a smile on his face he asked if I remembered him. I looked at him a moment and replied, "No, sir, I don't believe I do. Have we met somewhere?" He joyfully recounted walking into our store two years before, having a tract placed in his hand, and accepting Christ in that small room in the warehouse.

"Are you that man?" I asked.

"Yes," he replied. "I was passing through town and wanted to stop by to thank you from the bottom of my heart for what you did and what God has done. I have a good job, a happy home, and I am serving the Lord in my church and community."

All the store personnel were overjoyed as we all agreed how great our Lord is. God always knows the right moment, the right place, the right man. Do you see how marvelous are the ways of our Lord? Two people who had never met had prayed to God at the same hour. God is in the miracle-working business. All we need to do as Christians is to be willing and be available. God takes care of the rest!

Hell in the Home

A man wanting to sell all his furniture phoned our store and asked if I could come immediately to give him an estimate. When I arrived, a mover had already started loading the van. Sounds of crying children and a man and woman cursing could be heard from the house. The front door flew open and two small children ran toward me, pleading, "Please don't let Mamma and Daddy go!" Taking the children by the hands, I entered the house. The couple were in such a heated argument that they hardly noticed my presence.

I thought, *Lord, what is this? Hell's fury has surely enveloped these people.* It took several minutes to calm them before I could learn that their domestic problems had grown to such a proportion that separation seemed to be the only solution. There did not appear to be a thread of love or responsibility remaining, for they even planned to separate the children and send them to live with relatives.

Their heated argument had turned to stony silence and outward calm, so I seized upon the opportunity to suggest that since this was a lifelong decision affecting the lives of four people, nothing would be lost by spending a few more minutes discussing it quietly. They reluctantly agreed.

After asking the driver to wait in his truck, I then asked if they had a Bible in the house. The wife searched for a few minutes before finding one. I then opened the Bible and explained many Scriptures relating to the home and God's blessings on the home. We talked about the mother's and father's responsibilities in the home and with their children. I silently prayed for God to speak through me to those troubled people.

The fifth chapter of Ephesians provided words on how a man and a wife should love one another. Hesitantly, they began to discuss these things with me and relate the Scriptures to their own troubled lives. I felt the presence of God and knew he was in control. Their words softened, and the mother began to weep softly.

About this time the mover called in, saying he had been

waiting two hours and needed to complete his work. I assured him he would be paid for his time and asked him to return the furniture the following day. After another hour of talking and discussing Scripture, they confessed their love for one another. Finally, we all knelt and prayed. Each one turned over his burdens to the Lord and asked Christ to come into his heart and home as Lord and Master.

God knows just when and how to work things out according to his divine plan. When I entered that house, I found a family faced with a seemingly impossible situation—one which no power on earth could resolve; but "The things which are impossible with men, are possible with God" (Luke 18:27). I witnessed the miracle-working power of God to reestablish the home that was ordained of God before the church and the saving of a father and mother to bring up two precious children in a Christian environment.

Only God can take the hell out of a home and make it a place where Jesus abides. These are the words of Jesus: "And if a house be divided against itself, that house cannot stand" (Mark 3:25).

I have traveled over America and have seen the sorrow and successes of the homelife; and I am convinced that one of the greatest problems of our time is the home. If the homelife is right, all is right. The home is the center of everything.

No church life can rise higher than the homelife. One of the most precious things in this life is a home, with all the family on their way to heaven. The most horrible thing is an entire family on their way to hell. Let us remember that our national life will never rise above the homelife and never sink below it.

In my beloved state of Georgia, historians tell of a great Georgian, Henry W. Grady, journalist and orator, one who through his editorials and speeches helped promote the rebuilding of the South after the Civil War. While in Washington, D.C., looking at the United States Capitol for the first time, he remarked, "Here is the home of my nation; that building is the official home of the greatest nation God's eyes ever saw."

God has bountifully blessed our nation, and it is up to you and me to have homes that are pleasing to our Lord. Bible study and praying together are *musts* for family unity and a happy home.

The Blood of Three Men

One Christmas I was invited to speak to the tuberculosis patients in the prison ward of the state hospital that was located in my city. Although there were about sixty men in the ward, none of whom I knew, my attention was drawn to one in particular. He kept his eyes fixed on me as I gave a message on the birth of our Lord and Savior, Jesus Christ. To climax my message, I quoted some Scripture verses. Time was limited after the message because the lights would soon be turned out. The man slipped from his bed, walked up to me, placed his hand in mine, and said, "Sir, I'd give anything in the world if I could believe what you have said."

I thought as he was speaking to me, "My, what a delicate, soft hand for a man of his age." He appeared to be in his fifties. I asked him, "Why can't you believe, sir?" He replied, "I just can't lay hold of that, I can't get it, I can't believe it." As we were walking, he said it a second time.

Again I asked, "My friend, why can't you believe?" This time there was no reply. As we approached the door where I would have to leave him, my hand still clasped in his, for the third time he repeated his desire to believe.

I quoted John 3:36, "He that believeth on the Son hath everlasting life: and he that believeth not the Son shall not see life; but the wrath of God abideth on him." I told him he could believe God's Word, but he replied, "I'd give anything in this world, even my life, if I could believe that." He took his hand out of mine, raised three fingers and said, "But, sir, I have the blood of three men on my hands. I have murdered three times, and somehow I just can't lay hold of that which you have just said."

It was time to leave. Outside the building I spoke to the pastor who had invited me to be the guest speaker. "Brother

Pastor, did you hear what the man said?"

"Yes," he replied, "I heard him."

I said, "You know, something strange happened as this man spoke to me those three times and said he couldn't believe." Even though his hand was soft and tender as a baby's, his heart was as hard as a rock. He could not believe because his heart was hardened. Yes, the man had murdered three people. The feeling I had toward him was different from anyone I had ever witnessed to. I shall never forget him. Many times a man's heart is hardened, as was the heart of Pharaoh, because of the sin of unbelief. Unbelief is the sin that will cause any soul to go to eternity, lost without Christ, lost without hope.

I left the hospital, knowing in my mind and heart that here was a man who wanted to believe but who could not grasp the great truth because his heart was hardened. The sin of unbelief kept him from knowing Jesus as his Savior. I inquired about his condition, both physical and spiritual, a few months later, and was informed that he had accepted Christ as Savior before his death.

Beloved Son, Better Clothing, Beautiful Burial

The lovely city of Rome, Georgia, is located in the foothills of the Appalachian Mountains, about seventy miles northwest of Atlanta, the capital of Georgia. It is known as the "City of Seven Hills and Three Rivers" because of the topographic similarity to the seven hills of Rome, Italy. Today a magnificent sculpture of Capitoline, the wolf, and her adopted human babies, Romulus and Remus, stands in front of the Municipal Building. It was a gift from the citizens of Rome, Italy, to their "sister city," Rome, Georgia.

As in all cities, Rome has fortunate people and less fortunate people. One of our less fortunate was a man named Bob. I had seen Bob around town on many occasions but had never really become acquainted with him. Like the majority of people, I had never stopped to say hello or taken time to talk with him. His background, other than that he was poor, was unknown to me.

Jesus always had compassion for the poor and downtrodden. Galatians 2:10 says, "Only they would that we should remember the poor; the same which I also was forward to do." Then, "Inasmuch as ye have done it unto one of the least of these my brethren, ye have done it unto me" (Matt. 25:40).

Once, when Jesus was traveling to the city of Jericho, he encountered a large crowd that had been awaiting him. Among the crowd was a blind man who had heard of Jesus and his miracles. When he heard that Jesus was nearing the crowd, he cried out to him. Several in the crowd told him to be quiet and to hold his peace. They said, "No one's concerned about you!" But he cried louder; and as he heard Jesus come nearer, he cried, "Master." Jesus said, "What would thou have me do for thee?" The blind man said, "Restore my sight." Immediately his sight was restored. Bob was, in many ways, in the same circumstances as the blind man on the Jericho road—nobody cared whether he lived or died.

One day Bob joined me for coffee at a local soda fountain. He said he was ill and needed medical help but had no funds and no one to call upon for help. I said, "Bob, perhaps I can be of some help to you." As a Georgia state representative, possibly I could get him some assistance. Anyway, I promised Bob I would try.

After making inquiries and checking records, I discovered he had previously paid some Social Security and workman's compensation and therefore was eligible for help, small though it would be. He would have to go on welfare to receive any real help.

Several weeks went by after I had talked with the state welfare people. Bob called and said he had received a check from the welfare department; it was a little under $100, but he was so thrilled that he wept! The next time I saw Bob, he put his arms around me and said, "You are the only man that ever cared for me!" I was reminded of the Scripture that says, "I looked on my right hand, and beheld, but . . . no man cared for my soul" (Ps. 142:4). Here was a golden opportunity to prove my love, concern, and care for Bob. I decided to pursue the matter further. I called Bob's aunt, who had raised him. (His father and mother had died when he was quite young.) I told her I wanted to be kept informed of his progress. She was thrilled at my interest and concern and promised to keep in touch. She kept her promise and called me periodically.

Bob's health was deteriorating rapidly. One Saturday morning his aunt called and said, "E. B., I want you to come and see Bob and talk to him about the Lord. You're the only one he'll listen to because he knows you love and care about him." On the way to her house I prayed for God to give me the right words that Bob would understand and accept.

My visit to his aunt's house revealed that she was not only caring for Bob but also caring for her husband, who had just returned from an Atlanta hospital where he had undergone delicate surgery for cancer. Opening my Bible, I read some Scripture to them and then gave the Bible to Bob.

I asked him, "Can you read?"

"Well, a little," he said.

"Have you ever read John 3:16?" He said he thought so but was not sure, and he began stumbling his way through the verse. I took the Bible and read slowly, word by word, modifying it somewhat: "For God so loved Bob, not the world, but Bob, that he gave his only begotten son; that if Bob would believe, he could be saved!" The meaning of the Scripture seemed to take hold, and soon all four of us were on our knees. I prayed first; then his aunt and uncle prayed. I asked Bob if he would accept Jesus Christ as his personal Savior. He said, "I don't know how." I said, "If you truly believe in your heart the words I'm about to say, repeat them after me. Now if you don't mean business, don't repeat them." "Mr. Toles," he said, "I mean business."

Thoughtfully and sincerely he repeated these words, "Lord Jesus, I'm a sinner. I know I have sinned. I know I need salvation, and I know I can't save myself. I know that God loves me, and he gave his beloved Son, Jesus, to die for me. I know, Lord, that on some occasions I've been so despondent and desperate, I'm ashamed of it! I'm sorry for my sins. Lord, the best I know how, I want to ask you to forgive me, to come into my heart and save me; forgive me of all sin, and give me a home in heaven!" By this time, tears were rolling down Bob's cheeks; the Holy Spirit had knocked at his heart's door, and the beloved Son of God saved Bob! We stood up and locked arms around each other, rejoicing and praising God.

I said, "Bob, you know I love and care for you, but Jesus loves you much, much more than I or anyone else. I want you to go with me to praise the Lord in church." His aunt said that he did not have any clothes suitable for church. I asked Bob whether, if he had better clothes, he would be willing to go. He replied, "Yes." From my closet I selected and took to Bob a nice suit, several neckties, shirts, socks, and shoes— everything needed to dress him up for his public profession of faith.

Regretfully, Bob's steadily declining health prohibited him from ever going to church. He was unable to get out of bed, and his aunt finally had to put him in a nursing home. Soon his aunt's husband passed away. Naturally she was under a tremendous strain, losing her husband, having to make all the funeral arrangements, and still visiting Bob in the nursing home. However, she took the time to call and inform me that Bob was critically ill and asked if I would go see him. Of course I agreed.

The following day I went to Bob's room in the nursing home. He seemed near death but was conscious enough to recognize me. He held out his hand to me and big tears filled his eyes. He thanked me for all I had done, especially for the love and concern I had given him.

"Mr. Toles, you're the only person, other than my aunt and uncle, that ever really loved me. You are the only person that ever took time with me."

As we prayed, I felt that this would be our last prayer together. Before leaving, I told him I would see him tomorrow. Before nightfall his aunt called to tell me Bob had died. She said, "Bob would want you to conduct his funeral, and so do I. Will you do it?" I told her I certainly would.

I felt a great compassion for her. She had buried her husband on Sunday, the day Bob died, and now she had to bury her nephew. Such terrible strain and anguish! Of course I did everything possible to lighten her load and lift the burden, as did many of her other friends.

I will always remember that night when my wife and I went to the funeral home to pay our respects to Bob. I looked at the remains of my friend. He was clothed in the suit, necktie, and shirt I had given him. Among my thoughts as I looked upon him was, *There but by the grace of God lies E. B. Toles— my clothes—Bob's body.* I praised God and thanked him for the blessing Bob had been to me and the privilege of leading him to the Lord.

The next day at the funeral I gave a simple message and told some of Bob's background and how he had accepted the Lord as his Savior. Then I read from the Word, had a couple of hymns, and said a final prayer. On the way to the cemetery, the funeral director said to me, "Mr. Toles, that was a beautiful service. That man never knew the luxuries of this world." He wept when I told him the clothes Bob had on were given to him so he could attend church and make his public profession of faith, but he had never regained his health.

It was a beautiful afternoon, almost dusk, and the sun's rays were a golden hue. I looked at the family that had gathered and assured them of Bob's abiding home. I began to quote the Scriptures "I am the resurrection, and the life. He that believeth in me, though he were dead, yet shall he live" (John 11:25). "Let not your hearts be troubled, ye believe in God, believe also in me. In my father's house are many mansions" (John 14:1-2). Although he never knew of this world's luxuries, he was safe in the arms of Jesus for eternity. "Blessed are they that do his commandments, that they may have right to the tree of life, and may enter in through the gates into the city" (Rev. 22:14).

I am looking forward to meeting Bob again in heaven.

5

The Many Sides of Life

"But the word of God grew and multiplied" (Acts 12:24).

Several years ago I received a phone call from my good friend Dr. Grady Wilson, a member of the Billy Graham team, with whom I have had the privilege of working on several occasions. Grady was in Atlanta, Georgia, with Dr. Graham for a crusade. When Grady asked the long-distance operator for my telephone number, to his amazement she exclaimed, "I know that man! I have heard Mr. Toles preach many times and during one of his services I accepted the Lord into my life."

Grady was bubbling over with joy as he related this experience to me. "E. B., I knew you were dedicated to winning souls for Christ; but when your widespread efforts are acclaimed by a chance encounter, it just proves that if we plant the seed, the harvest will be great."

Luke 15:10 says, "Likewise, I say unto you, there is joy in the presence of the angels of God over one sinner that repenteth." It is a precious experience when the Lord reveals what has transpired with the sown seed over the years. Once a professor approached me and asked if I remembered him. Regretfully, I had to admit I did not. He introduced himself and his two sons and said, "I heard you were in town and I wanted to see you. Perhaps you may recall conducting a revival meeting in our church many years ago. During that meeting I was saved. I was a young man of about twenty, and soon after that I entered college. Unfortunately, many of my college friends made fun of my religious beliefs. Some of these boys had attended your meeting with me. There were many difficult trials and enticements, but my conviction was strong enough to withstand. So I owe you thanks and a debt of gratitude— first, because I found Christ through you; and secondly, as a result of that, I now have a Christian home with a wife and two children who are saved."

What brings joy and happiness? Doing for others. Helping people to find Christ as Savior pays greater dividends than can ever be tallied. God has opened doors for me to preach the good news. When those who hear God's Word accept him into their lives, like the young college boy, what occurs is nothing short of a miracle. The event was simply God-ordained, God-planned, and God-provided.

"Be Thou Clean" (Matt. 8:3)

We never know what words will reach the heart and soul of the unsaved. Usually we rely on the Scriptures; but the Lord can use anything, even a soap commercial that I heard one day on the television and from which I chose the words of the advertisement, "Clean Clear Through," for a sermon topic.

The church was filled with young people during a revival service planned just for them. They had various musical groups to sing and an extremely talented young man at the piano.

My message was centered on Jesus Christ's cleansing us from all sin, and I illustrated it with the story of Jesus healing the leper (Matt. 8:1-4). During the invitation a young girl about eighteen years old came forward and joyously proclaimed, "I feel clean clear through. It took more than a soap product to cleanse me—it's the blood of Jesus Christ. Praise God! I *am* clean clear through."

Other young people started coming forward to claim salvation and to rededicate their lives. Then, to my amazement, the young man at the piano came forward and said to me, "Mr. Toles, I've been singing and playing praises to Jesus for years but have never really known him as Lord and Savior. I, too, want to be made clean clear through."

Through the testimony of those who had come forward, many others followed, wanting to be made clean. Truly, the

Lord can use anything to his glory. I felt led to close the service with the words of the prophet Isaiah, "Wash you, make you clean; put away the evil of your doings from before mine eyes; cease to do evil" (Isa. 1:16).

The Executive Made the Right Choice

The Christian must not yield to desires of worldly allurement. Striving to be Christlike should be the object of his life. Speaking at a church in a northern city, I used this as a theme for one of my sermons. Wanting to appeal to the businessmen in the audience, I illustrated the message from my own experience in the furniture business. I compared the beautiful glossy exterior of veneered furniture to the thin coating of Christianity many of us wear. We seem to have Christian luster and polish, reflecting a spiritual glow; but, like veneered furniture, some of us are rough and unfinished inside. Christianity to some is just a thin coating. Often the success of suppressing an inner desire depends upon the depth of our faith and our belief in God's Word. "For we are labourers together with God . . . I have laid the foundation, and another buildeth thereon. But let every man take heed how he buildeth thereupon" (1 Cor. 3:9–10). "Let no man deceive himself. If any man among you seemeth to be wise in this world, let him become a fool, that he may be wise" (1 Cor. 3:18).

Later that evening a member of the congregation came to my hotel room and asked if we could discuss a decision he had to make regarding his job. He had been offered a promotion that could lead to one of the highest positions in the company and a raise in salary amounting to many thousands of dollars, but it would entail social activities that would include alcoholic beverages. His real question seemed to be whether he could work in such an atmosphere and still profess and maintain his Christian principles.

It would not have been feasible for me to make that decision for him. I could only give him some spiritual truths. To him I said, "First, you belong to Jesus; therefore you should obey him and let his word be your law. Second, let his will be your

will. Third, if you belong to God, the Scripture teaches us to
'Trust in the Lord . . . and lean not unto thine own understanding. In all thy ways acknowledge him, and he shall direct thy
paths' (Prov. 3:5–6). The fourth thing is, if you belong to him,
you need to make your decision known to all men that Christ
makes the difference in your life and that you will abide with
the Lord Jesus, come what may."

I suggested that we pray together, asking God for divine
guidance and wisdom in the decision. I assured him that if
he would listen to God, the Holy Spirit would direct him in
the right path. Before leaving the room, he decided to tell
his wife that his decision had been made. He was going to
be faithful to the Lord and to his church and tell his company
he could not take the promotion because of Christian convictions.

Some months later I received a letter from that man. After
he had informed the company officials that he could not accept
the position under such circumstances, the president of the
company, who had recently become a Christian, requested
he come to the home office. The president congratulated him
on his decision and offered him another promotion equivalent
in status and salary to the original offer, but without any demands that would be offensive to his Christian beliefs. Reflecting on how close he had come to making the wrong decision,
he praised God and noted, "If a man is faithful and true to
God, God will in his own time and due course work it out;
God will never fail you if you will be faithful to him."

My reply to his letter was directed to the Scripture found
in Joshua 1:8-9: "This book of the law shall not depart out of
thy mouth; but thou shalt meditate therein day and night, that
thou mayest observe to do according to all that is written
therein: for then thou shalt make thy way prosperous, and
then thou shalt have good success. Have not I commanded
thee? Be strong and of a good courage; be not afraid, neither
be thou dismayed: for the Lord thy God is with thee whither-
soever thou goest."

"Restitution"

"And if it be stolen from him, he shall make restitution unto the owner thereof" (Ex. 22:12).

We must sincerely attempt to right things with our fellow-man before we can expect God to help us. God can make us recall forgotten injustices and other hurts we have inflicted on our fellowman when we are searching our hearts and souls to come clean with the Lord. The Lord dealt sharply with me over a long forgotten incident that occurred when I was out of the will of God and not ready to surrender all.

I had not been in the furniture business long when we had an exhibit at an adjoining county fair. My boss had asked me to look after things at the fair exhibit. Working with me was a man who was not a Christian and to whom I had never witnessed about the Lord.

This was in the early 1940s, before World War II ended. Merchandise was not plentiful, but it was a buyer's market. Radios were in great demand in the days before television. We allowed the customers a ten- or twenty-dollar trade-in on their old radios. One day we sold some of the old radios for $200. My co-worker said, "Now look, E. B., no one knows anything about this; we could have just given the radios away. Let's not turn this money in. You take half, I'll take half, and we will pocket $100 each." I was not hard to convince, and I agreed to the proposition.

Some years later, in business for myself, I began searching for God's will for my life. My prayer was, "Lord, reveal anything that is wrong in my life." It was a soul-searching experience. The one hundred dollars came before me. There was no plausible explanation or excuse; I had absolutely stolen the one hundred dollars. I told my wife of this. She knew I had to have help, and she joined me in prayer about the matter. I prayed for a solid week, day and night, for courage to go to my former boss and confess the wrong I had done. It was hard for me to face him because he trusted me. I had known the combination to the safe and had a key to the cash drawer. He was convinced I was an honest man. It was going to be humiliating and painful, but I knew I must tell him the whole story.

Finally, I got up the courage, called him, and made arrangements to meet him that evening. Before leaving home, I wrote a check for one hundred dollars and put it in my coat pocket. Upon arriving at his store, I greeted him and said, "I owe you a hundred dollars." He opened the big ledger, turned to the "T's" and said, "No, I don't find any sheet here, E. B. I think you have cleared up everything."

"No, sir, I owe you a hundred dollars."

"Well, it's not on the books."

It took me a while to confess what had happened and how I had taken one hundred dollars for sale of the used merchandise. "Mr. _____, I've been praying and asking God to put his finger on anything wrong in my life. I don't want to leave one stone unturned; God convicted me of this sin. Please forgive me."

He turned to me and said, "I'll have to admit one thing, E. B.; it took guts to admit what you did and I shall always admire you for this. It took a big man to do what you have done."

"Let me assure you, Mr. _____, I didn't do it; it took a week of praying to get up the courage to come here and tell you this, but God provided the courage."

What a lesson I learned from the experience! I felt a ton had rolled off my shoulders; a weight had lifted from me. I believe in restitution with all of my heart. We all have wrongs that need to be made right. Search your heart and remember these words: "He that handleth a matter wisely shall find good: and whoso trusteth in the Lord, happy is he" (Prov. 16:20).

Condemned

"He that believeth on him is not condemned; but he that believeth not is condemned already, because he hath not believed in the name of the only begotten Son of God" (John 3:18).

Appointed chairman of a special committee as a Georgia legislator, I had the duty of visiting the state penal institutions throughout the state of Georgia. This involved meeting with those whose duties were to oversee the prisoners and to talk with scores of men and women who were serving out their sentences, some condemned to death.

One cannot help but reflect on the many paths those people took to their common destination. Did they find their path without assistance? Did another point the way? Was there someone who could have diverted those fateful steps? Most of those prisoners felt that the path they had traveled ended when the bars closed behind them; but I was shown the final destination for some, and it will forever be ingrained in my memory. In Georgia it has been several years since the last execution in the electric chair, but it is still ready for use. I asked the chaplain of the state prison if he would guide our committee through the final steps for a condemned man.

We entered an elevator and rode to the fifth floor. There were no stairs leading beyond the fourth floor. Immediately to our right, as the door opened, were five small cells just large enough for a bunk bed and a commode. These cells were known as "death row"; each one contained a condemned man. As we passed each one, I was allowed to speak briefly to him, and I used the opportunity to say a few words about Jesus' love for all mankind—his eternal salvation, free to all who asked him.

Passing the last cell, the chaplain asked us to look up. A small opening in the roof, covered by iron bars, offered the prisoner his last opportunity to view the sky. This was referred to as the last look upward. Ten steps further and we reached the door of the death room—gray walls, a wall telephone with direct connection to the governor's office in case of a last-minute reprieve, and, directly ahead of us, the chair!

At this point the chaplain would pause with the prisoner and read some Scripture. Then a few steps more to the chair. I sat down, felt the heavy straps, and turned to look at large electrical switches behind the chair. Before the switches are pulled, the condemned man is asked if he has anything to say; then a black cap is placed over his head.

Speaking to my fellow committeemen and the chaplain, I quoted John 3:18 and wondered aloud how many condemned men through the ages would have chosen another path if they had conceived beforehand the meaning of "condemned to death."

People must be aware that one does not have to commit murder to be condemned. We are condemned already, according to God's Word in John 3:18. But thank God for his love, a love so great that he sent his son to take our sins upon himself and die in our place so that we might have eternal life.

What is required of us? We must trust Jesus and believe on him. "Whosoever believeth in him should not perish, but have eternal life" (John 3:15).

"Today"

God places people in our pathway.

During my college and Bible school training, I asked the dean of the school to refer me to a local doctor. The dean told me of one he had known all his life and said, "E. B., I want you to witness to this man. He is a friend of my family, but I never have been able to witness effectively to him. Perhaps you, as a layman, may have the key that will open the door to his heart."

We bowed our heads and prayed for him. On the way to the doctor's office, I uttered a prayer for a man I had never met. He gave me a checkup and wrote a prescription. Noticing my information card, which stated my age and that I was a businessman back in school studying for the ministry, he said, "You know, this is very unusual, Mr. Toles. A man of your age in college. What about your business back home?"

I quickly replied, "Doctor, I reached the conclusion not too many months ago that the most important thing in life isn't how much money I make; it is what I do for Jesus Christ."

This brought on an interesting conversation, and we talked about the Scriptures for an hour. As I was leaving, he placed his hand in mine and said: "You know, I like what you have said and want to talk with you some more. Come back every other day; let me give you some vitamin shots which you need; and we'll talk some more about religion." I assured him that I would be happy to.

On my second visit to his office, I took a Gideon personal worker's New Testament and underscored Romans 10:9-10 and John 3:16. I asked him to promise that he would read them, and he said he would. He kept the little Bible; and each time I went back to his office we discussed the Scriptures. He was as interested in the Scripture as he was in my physical condition. After two or three occasions, I was convinced that God had placed him in my pathway. There was no doubt about it. I told the dean of the school, and he agreed that God was working. I asked my family back home to pray for that doctor. We became great friends; and he took me to visit in homes and to the hospital on several occasions. He had many questions about religion, some of which I could not answer; but I did the best I could. Pointing to a picture of his son one day, he asked, "Why did God take my only boy?" (His son died while attending medical college.) I could not answer that; all I could say to him was that God never makes a mistake.

There is another true lesson I learned from that experience. Regardless of wealth, skill, knowledge, and wisdom, when dealing with God we are all on the same level. There is no difference.

It was getting close to time for the semester to end. I asked him to have lunch with me before I returned home. As I entered his office on the given day and time to meet him, he was reading in a medical magazine about the Great Physician. He put his arm around me and made a statement that I shall never forget. "Son, I've saved hundreds of lives on the operating table and accumulated a vast amount of wealth; I'm an old man now; but I'm the most miserable man that you've ever met. I'm a miserable wretch."

It was apparent that I had been dealing with a man who had a longing in his heart for Christ. It was difficult to get to the point where I could invite him to allow Jesus to come into his heart. I was praying for that very moment and was leaving it in God's hand because I believed the Holy Spirit in his own way and in due time would provide the right time and place. While we were at the table discussing Christianity, I said, "Doctor, you need to prepare to meet God *today*." When I said those words, I noticed tears in his eyes. I knew the Holy Spirit was speaking to him. He said, "I'd give anything in the world if I had the peace in my heart that you have."

Turning to Philippians 4, I read the sixth and seventh verses: "Be careful for nothing; but in every thing by prayer and supplication with thanksgiving let your requests be made known unto God. And the peace of God, which passeth all understanding, shall keep your hearts and minds through Christ Jesus." I said, "Doctor, here's the way to peace, and it's through Christ Jesus."

When I spoke those words, tears rolled down his cheeks, and he said, "Wait a minute, I do not want to create a scene here; let's get back to my office." It is wonderful that the Lord gave me just the right Scriptures at the right time!

We returned to his office. Again making reference to the peace he had been searching for all these years, he turned his chair around, took me by the hand, and said, "Will you pray with me?" We went to our knees and prayed. I prayed first; and after my prayer, the doctor lifted his heart to God. Then he asked, "Mr. Toles, will God forgive me for my wickedness?"

"Doctor, 1 John 1:9 tells us that the blood of Jesus Christ cleanses us from all sin and unrighteousness." He prayed and asked again. "Will God forgive my sins?" I kept insisting that the blood of Jesus Christ would forgive all sins. I quoted words from the Old Testament: "Though your sins be as scarlet, they shall be as white as snow; though they be as red like crimson, they shall be as wool" (Isa. 1:18).

He was beginning to understand. The Holy Spirit was working. It was like dynamite! The power and love of God became a reality to him. He arose, praising God, and said, "Jesus Christ is my Lord and I'm accepting him and asking forgiveness for my sins. I know that Jesus Christ has come into my heart and saved me!"

The Lord Jesus said, "Him that cometh to me I will in no wise cast out" (John 6:37). With that assurance he was totally convinced of his salvation. He walked over to the wash basin to wash his face because he had wept so bitterly. After we had rejoiced together, he made this statement: "You know, Mr. Toles, this is what I've been looking for all my life. Now I have the peace of God in my heart. I'm going home to tell my wife what has happened. If I go to sleep tonight never to awake, it will be all right; I know I will go to heaven."

We were together rejoicing until 5 o'clock. The doctor went home and told his wife what had happened that afternoon. He had a social engagement that evening but canceled it, saying he was going to bed early.

The doctor died in his sleep that night.

The next morning before daybreak, the dean of the school came to my door, woke me, and said, "Mr. Toles, Dr. _____ is dead." I thought I was having a nightmare.

I said, "What are you saying?" "Dr. _____ died in his sleep last night." The dean was not aware of what had happened the day before. He did not know that the doctor had accepted Jesus. I then told him the story, and he said, "Oh, praise God, Brother Toles, certainly our prayers have been answered and God's timetable to the hour, to the day, has been fulfilled. Thank God that you got there in time."

That experience changed my entire life. How important it is to grasp every opportunity when God opens the door. Never did I realize as I witnessed to the doctor that it would be his last day on earth. When dealing with an unsaved person one never knows if it is to be his last opportunity.

"Behold, now is the accepted time; behold, now is the day of salvation" (2 Cor. 6:2).

6

Incidents on the Road of Life

Prayer

"Ye have not, because ye ask not" (Jas. 4:2).

Many wonderful years had passed; and I was happy in the Lord's work, preaching God's Word where God opened the door. I had speaking engagements booked a year in advance and was praying that God would give me the greatest year of my lay work. Then once again he saw fit to test my faith and permitted a serious illness to plague my body.

I could not continue with the commitments I had made. Yet with determination, I held on to the promise of God and trusted him. Again the words of Job came to me: "Though he slay me, yet will I trust in him" (Job 13:15). I recalled the undeniable truth in the words "If all were easy, if all were bright, where would the cross be, where would be the fight?" But I had learned that in the hard places, God gives chances for proving what he can do. That is exactly what happened to me at that crucial point in my life and ministry. God proved what he could do.

Each week my body continued to weaken, and I soon realized I must see a physician. A pastor-friend, knowing of the many physical problems I had had in the past, insisted that I see his doctor, a well-known urologist. During my three-day stay in the hospital, numerous x rays and tests were made. The doctor advised me to go home and get my business in order. He told me to return in three days, prepared for an operation to remove my right kidney, which could be cancerous. During those three days and nights I learned what it was to fast and pray. If there was ever a time in my life when I fervently prayed, that was the time. My prayer was simple but very definite. I had three requests: "(1) O Lord, if it can be thy will, spare me this operation; (2) may I not have cancer of the kidney; and (3) let me live. My desire is to live that I might preach the gospel and be your servant and continue my work as a layman."

After I checked into the hospital, the doctor came into the room to reassure me that everything would be all right. I said, "Doctor, wait a minute. I want to tell you something. I've been praying for these three days and nights and I don't believe I need a kidney operation." He quickly replied, "With all the tests that we've done, there isn't one chance in a thousand that we have missed." "All right, doctor, but I'm still holding on to God, I still have faith, and I'll take my chances on my one against a thousand."

It is interesting how God prepares everything to the very moment, the hour, the day. I have said on many occasions that God's timetable in my life has been so important. While the orderly was preparing me for the preliminary cystoscopic operation, he mentioned that he was studying for the ministry. As he was about to take me from my room, I said, "I want to pray one more time." He said, "You know, sir, I'm glad to hear you say that. Would you mind if I joined you in a prayer?" "I'd be delighted," I replied. He got on his knees beside my bed to join my wife and me in prayer.

I was in the operating room approximately one hour; and when I came to from the sedation, the doctor was standing over me saying, "You do not have to have surgery." Still under the influence of the medication, I did not fully grasp what he was saying. Later he came to my room and informed me that I was not going to have the operation because I was born with only one kidney; I had no kidney on the right side. They could not remove what was not there! Praise God! You may say that was luck. I say not! It was a miracle, a direct answer to prayer. I had prayed a definite prayer, and God had answered that prayer. The three petitions were answered: I am still alive, I am still preaching, and I do not have cancer. That is enough to make any man shout "Hallelujah" and want to serve God!

The orderly came to my room three days later and told me I had all the doctors talking about my case, and they were confused. One of them said they should write a book about me because all the tests resulted in the same diagnosis; yet all had been proved wrong. I remember I said to tell them not to worry about writing a book about me, to just let me out of the hospital. I was reminded of the story of Lazarus raised from the dead. The Scripture said, "Loose him, and let him go" (John 11:44).

As the same orderly took me in a wheelchair to my car, he said, "Mr. Toles, you know, when I got on my knees to pray beside your bed in that hospital room, *we prayed that kidney clean out of you.*" Praise the Lord! He never fails us. "Knowing that he which raised up the Lord Jesus shall raise up us also by Jesus, and shall present us with you" (2 Cor. 4:14).

After a few months' rest and medication, I was back on my job again. Paul, in 1 Corinthians 2:9-10, said, "But as it is written, Eye hath not seen, nor ear heard, neither have entered into the heart of man, the things which God hath prepared for them that love him. But God hath revealed them unto us by his Spirit: for the Spirit searcheth all things, yea, the deep things of God." That experience was another of those deeply revealing experiences in my life, and I praise God. I asked and I received! Oh, how sweet and precious is the Lord! The songwriter put it to words: "Just when I need him most; Jesus is near, to comfort, and cheer." I join the psalmist of old: "Because thy lovingkindness is better than life, my lips shall praise thee" (Ps. 63:3).

Prayer Warrior

Have you ever been in the presence of a person and you feel as though you can almost reach out and touch the gates of heaven? I have. I want to share with you a great experience about one of God's chosen prayer warriors. He was a custodian of a great university in another state. He had never attended college, but he had great wisdom; and I learned much from his life. No man is gauged by God for his elegance or his orthodox belief or practice, but by his prayer.

Knowing this man and his great faith, I went to his home, wanting him to pray for me and with me. He said, "E. B., come with me." We walked down to a creek bank on his small farm, where he had been born and had lived for sixty-five years. One could not help but note that the path was well trodden.

Every day before sunrise, regardless of the weather, he always walked down to the creek, got on his knees, and prayed to God. He prayed not only for himself but also for the university and its students and for others with whom he had come in contact. It was widely known that if you wanted someone to pray for you, someone who knew how to get in touch with God, you should talk to that man.

As we came to the place, I was awed by its natural beauty. There was a huge, flat rock embedded in the earth at the curve of the creek. Large oak trees with limbs upstretched to heaven surrounded the rock. Strangely, the limbs left an opening to the sky, directly over the rock. On that rock we knelt to pray. The man said, "Look upward." I did so and was amazed to see the warm morning sun shining directly on us through the opening in the trees. I am certain God had designed that little place especially for the man of prayer.

As we prayed, I heard that dear soul pour out his heart to God. The words of James 4:2, "Ye have not, because ye ask not," became a revelation to me that day. As I was kneeling and praying with that man, my heart was lifted until it seemed I was in the very presence of God!

Some years later, I went back to that university town on business and had an occasion to meet the president of the school. "Is the custodian still on the job?" I asked. A smile came across the president's face as he told me that the custodian had retired, but the students and faculty had insisted he visit the university campus each day to counsel and pray with them as he had been doing all these years. To them he was one of the most important men on the campus. The president continued his praise of the man by saying, "That man is one of the greatest prayer warriors that ever walked the grounds of this university. Students, faculty, and administrators admire and love him."

He said, "Let me tell you more about that fellow. Did you know, Mr. Toles, that he is invited to churches for miles in every direction by pastors of all denominations. They invite him for one reason: the opportunity to hear him pray. When the word gets around that he will be in their midst on Sunday morning, the church is usually packed. I believe they come to hear him pray, perhaps more than to hear the sermon." Prayer is wealth. It is to the Christian what capital is to the businessman.

Much has been said about prayer in sermons and in the Bible. Prayer is the most powerful form of energy that one can generate. I wonder if any of us really know how to pray. Surely we all pray when emergencies confront us, but is that really talking with God?

Once, while I was on an airplane, flying at about thirty thousand feet, something went temporarily wrong with the motor; and I thought we were going to crash. My heart seemed to leap into my throat, and I began to pray. Believe me, it is not hard to pray when emergencies come! We landed without incident, and my thanks went up to the good Lord! Later I told my wife about this, and she quickly said I had prayed a "scared prayer." Perhaps it was a scared prayer, but it is glorious that we have a Savior to call upon in all circumstances! Real prayer is needed and must take over in our lives and in the life of our nation. We need to pray for the outpouring of the Holy Spirit to take over our ship; for we are small, and the sea is stormy.

Dwight L. Moody once said, "The beginning of greatness is to be little, the increase of greatness is to be less, and the perfection of greatness is to be nothing." This is Christian progress. When we read in the book of Luke, what do we find?

We find a story of perpetual progress. Acts 4:4 and 6:7 are the same: progress and victory ring out in every chapter.

I was sitting on the platform with one of our great religious leaders not long ago. He turned to me and said, "Toles, I'm convinced we have today the greatest church buildings, the greatest music, choirs, and musical programs; but there's one thing we do not have, and this is the power of God upon us."

"What do you attribute this to?"

"It's the lack of prayer. We need a new spiritual injection from God, one that will give us new and more vitality, new vision, and a better view of our own sinful condition. Most of all, we need to hear the voice of God in prayer for victory through Jesus Christ our Lord. You recall what he promised in his Word in Mark 11:24: 'Therefore I say unto you, What things soever ye desire, when ye pray, believe that ye receive them, and ye shall have them.' " I am convinced that the reason we Christians are weak, shallow, inconsistent, and unconcerned is lack of prayer life.

Jesus prayed before all great crises. He prayed before choosing the twelve disciples. He prayed before the Sermon on the Mount. He prayed before starting on an evangelistic tour. He prayed before his anointing with the Holy Spirit. He prayed before his entrance upon his public ministry. He prayed in the garden of Gethsemane. He prayed before the culmination of his life on the cross. James 5:16 teaches us, "The effectual, fervent prayer of a righteous man availeth much." How many of us realize the tremendous power in earnest praying?

If we expect God to listen to us, my friend, we must be in tune with him. Someone once said, "We need God the Father to pray to; we need Jesus Christ the Son to pray through; and we need the Holy Spirit to pray in." It is the prayer to God, the Father, through Jesus Christ, the Son, under the guidance and power of the Holy Spirit that God answers.

Moses, Abraham, and Jacob were men of prayer. Hannah was a woman of prayer. She prayed for a son, and God gave her Samuel. Elijah prayed and closed up heaven for three years and six months. Then he prayed again, and the heavens gave rain to the earth. Elijah prayed and brought down fire on Mount Carmel. He prayed, and life was restored to a dead child. Daniel prayed, and God stopped the jaws of the lions. We are not told that Jesus ever taught his disciples how to preach, but he did teach them how to pray. Devils tremble, thrones crumble, and empires topple, in answer to those who know how to prevail with God in prayer. We should be so well versed in the Scripture that we have at the tips of our tongues the promise which exactly meets our needs. Let us never forget that the promises of God are longer than life, brighter than sin, deeper than the grave, and higher than the clouds. God help us to become a praying people!

The apostle Peter, while in prison awaiting death at Herod's hand, spent his time talking with God. The members of the church spent their time doing the same thing. "Peter therefore was kept in prison: but prayer was made without ceasing of the church unto God for him" (Acts 12:5). The Lord heard the prayers of the faithful and decided to save Peter for further work. He sent an angel into the prison, and the angel freed Peter. The people were astonished; but they should not have been, for God's power is unlimited. What a beautiful and wonderful story!

All of us are weak and doubting at times; and whenever I feel this and wonder if I am getting through to God, I read Acts 12 to reassure myself and revitalize my faith in the power of prayer. You should try it, too. The Bible is filled with powerful stories such as these: God's people talking to him and God's taking action!

The Invitation Stands!

For many years I served with the Gideons, an organization of Christian businessmen who devote a good deal of their time to speaking in churches, giving of their finances, and helping to raise funds to purchase and distribute Bibles to hotels, motels, and schools throughout the world. It was a great joy to be involved in that work with Christian businessmen from all walks of life. I served as state chaplain of the Georgia Gideons for four years, and I was thus afforded many great opportunities to meet outstanding Christian businessmen throughout the nation.

Some years ago, I was invited to speak to a Christian businessmen's conference in another state. After my message, a businessman asked if, in the near future, I would visit a certain children's home for a four-day speaking engagement. The date was agreed upon. Knowing very little about the home, I went there with a simple message of the Bible and Christ.

The first night, fifty children came forward and accepted Christ as their Savior. The second night the auditorium was filled to capacity, and many children came forward when the invitation was given. After the service the administrator of the school called me into his office and said, "We don't believe in the way you handled your services here tonight." I asked, "What do you mean? Don't believe I'm preaching the Bible?" "Yes," he said, "I didn't say you were not preaching the Bible, but I'm not so sure we agree with this business of giving an invitation and asking people to come forward to accept Christ."

Never had anyone said this to me in all my preaching experiences! I looked him straight in the eye and said, "Sir, let me tell you something. I was invited to preach the gospel, isn't that right?" He agreed. "One cannot preach the gospel and just walk away without giving an invitation for people to accept Christ. I thought this was the reason for my coming." He said, "Not exactly. We just wanted you to talk to the students. I'll think about this and talk with you again tomorrow."

I was adamant about giving an invitation. Dwight L. Moody said that his greatest mistake was the failure to give an invitation at a service he had held on the night of the Chicago fire, in which many people died. I was *not* going to make that mistake.

Before the service the next night a devout Christian teacher who had been at the services sent word for me to come to her office. When I arrived she said, "Oh, praise God, Mr. Toles! We've had many people talk to these children, but none of them ever gave an invitation to accept Jesus except you. You're saying what has been needed here for many, many months; and I want to tell you not to surrender your convictions to the administrator."

I said, "I told him last night that I would give an invitation and preach Jesus straight from the Word, or I would leave." She said, "You stick to your guns; don't give up." We made a vow to pray about this matter.

That afternoon I met with the administrator again and discussed the issue. That night I said to the Lord, "You've brought me a long way to preach the Bible to this home. If I am not allowed to preach with no strings attached, Lord, I shall have to leave the job unfinished." When the administrator and I met the next morning, he had changed his mind. I praised God for the answer to prayer. Before the conclusion of the services, hundreds had accepted Christ.

I went away praising the Lord for the prayers and encouragement from the Christian teacher and remembering the words of Jesus: "Again I say unto you, That if two of you shall agree on earth as touching any thing that they shall ask, it shall be done for them of my Father which is in heaven. For where two or three are gathered together in my name, there am I in the midst of them" (Matt. 18:19-20).

Overwhelmed by God's Presence

Have you ever been alone and suddenly felt God's presence so strongly that you were simply overwhelmed? One Sunday morning I was to preach in a large church in another city a good distance from Rome. I had to leave home before sunrise. Pondering on my sermon and being mindful that in a few hours I was to be God's spokesman to thousands of people brought to my heart and mind the need for fervent prayer in my own life.

Driving in an eastward direction and praying out loud in my car, I looked up; and it seemed that the beautiful sunrise leaped forth out of the earth. The sun's piercing ray from the brilliant sunrise seemed to serve as a searchlight into my soul. I became conscious of my unworthiness. I was going to represent the King of kings and Lord of lords. A sense of deep conviction of the need of prayer in preparation for that particular day somehow caused me to quickly turn my car off the highway onto a little dirt road, drive far into the forest, and stop under a large tree. With my Bible in my hand, I knelt in prayer and supplication to the Lord. I was overwhelmed by the presence and power of God for those moments, and words are inadequate to describe what happened in my soul.

Suddenly I felt the warm golden rays of sunlight shine upon my face; and, looking around, I was cognizant of the beautiful forest, grass, and trees. Even the chirp of the little birds God had commanded to rest in the trees over my head was music to my soul. My inadequacy evaporated, my apprehension was gone, and I felt completely engulfed with God's power and love.

As I approached the car, there was a large snake crawling toward me. I froze in my tracks for a moment; then, recovering from the fright of the serpent, I quickly stepped around it, got into my car, and continued to the church, aware that many would be listening as the sermon was broadcast by radio.

I began to think of the first few chapters in the Bible. My mind centered around God's creative art described in Genesis, and I recalled the temptation of Eve in the Garden of Eden. The serpent, Satan's tool, was cursed and became God's illustration in nature of the effects of sin.

In spite of the preparation and outline, my sermon subject changed as I made my way toward the city where I was to preach that morning. Again I was compelled to stop my car. I jotted down a few thoughts on the back of an envelope: the subtle, sultry, slimy, subduing serpent and his poison as a symbol of sin—compared to the simple salvation, security, and supreme love of our Savior. I was ready to preach when I arrived at that church! Praise the Lord! God did a marvelous thing in that morning service. Again I was overwhelmed with the presence and power of God.

No man can change my mind about my God. I know the Lord works in mysterious ways; sometimes it takes a snake to set our souls afire for the Lord. Sometimes God puts a politician up a sycamore tree (Luke 19) before he can speak to him. I confess here and now that I confirm what the apostle Paul said: "For I am not ashamed of the gospel of Christ: for it is the power of God unto salvation to everyone that believeth; to the Jew first, and also to the Greek" (Rom. 1:16). It works, and it is a glorious experience to see, feel, and know the presence and power of God.

God's Blessings Abound

One of my dearest friends was a pastor, who often visited in my home. Upon occasion, we discussed my ministry, my life, and my future. He and many other pastors gave me good advice, for which I shall always be grateful. My friend insisted that I never become an ordained minister.

"Now, E. B., don't let anyone ever tell you to be ordained, because you are not the type of man to be a pastor. Your lay type of ministry will be used greatly. There is a great need for men like you, who are willing to take their time and give it to preaching the gospel. People will listen to you who wouldn't listen to me as a pastor." At that time I felt that he was trying to be kind and was perhaps overexpressing his views. As I look back over the years, I know he was right.

I recall when I was invited to Charlotte, North Carolina, to be the featured speaker for the Christian businessmen's organization. We had a great group of husbands and wives the first night. One of the couples was Dr. Billy Graham's father and mother. Dr. Graham's mother called me aside after my message and said, "Young man, I want to tell you something. I had heard a little about your coming; but since I have heard your message, I want you to remember this as long as you are in the Lord's work; don't you ever let anyone put preacher on your name." Then Mr. Graham said, "We have preachers. What we need is Christian businessmen who believe and have a message to tell, men who are willing to go as laymen and speak throughout the country as Christian businessmen. People will listen many times to a layman when they will not go to church or hear what the preacher says."

There is no doubt in my mind about the calling of God in my life. It is a strange experience when men get that call from God. He puts something into their souls and in their bones that cannot be explained, but it is there; and they are acutely aware of it. I know that God called me as a lay speaker. He has a place of service for you. Be natural; remember that God made no other person just like you, but do your best, whatever your calling may be. Dwight L. Moody once said, "Do what you can, where you are, with what you have." I have found that people, regardless of their knowledge, like and appreciate simplicity.

The point is that God has called me to do a job. No one can take my place; nor can I fill the place of another Christian. If I fail God, then my job will never be done on this earth according to God's will. Likewise, God has a plan for every Christian's life, and perhaps this is why so many Christians are unhappy. They have never found their places in life and in the will of God.

The late Dr. Arthur Moore, Methodist bishop of Georgia, whom I knew and had heard preach many times, told of an experience he had when he first started out as a young minister. A woman came to him during a revival meeting and said, "Young man, I'm praying to the Lord about your ministry. O God, make this young preacher a surprise to himself, an astonishment to the congregation, a glory to God, and a terror to the devil!" I said, "Ah, not bad. This is good for any man who preaches God's Word."

During all my years of preaching, I have been careful that no one erroneously assumes that I am trying to take the place of a minister. God has given all of us certain jobs to do. The Scripture says that some are to be evangelists, some prophets, some teachers.

I would have gotten out of the will of God if I had listened to the persuasion of people. On several occasions during the past twenty-five years, I have had a delegation come to me and ask that I serve as their pastor. That was not my call; I am convinced of that. Many times when I go to a church to preach, after the service people will come to me and say, "Why aren't you a pastor?" I have even had people to say to me, "You look like a preacher." Well, I have never yet figured out how a preacher is supposed to look.

After all these years of working with preachers in various denominations, I never cease to thank God for their kindnesses toward me. God bless them; I love each one who is true to God's word, regardless of his denomination. Those people in full-time service for our Lord find it difficult at times. They need our prayers.

7

Modern-Day Pentecost

When we read the record of the early Christian church, we are aware that tremendous things happened. That small group of people changed the course of history. Acts 2:1 tells us they were "all with one accord in one place." Gathering together was good, but the key here is the three words "with one accord." The Bible tells us that they were all filled with the Holy Ghost when the power of God descended upon them in mighty force. At Pentecost there were those who mocked them, even accused them of being full of wine; but Peter said unto them, "This is that which was spoken by the prophet Joel" (Acts 2:16).

For many years I prayed to be a part of such an experience. It did not occur among the "high and mighty," but among simple people with few worldly goods—people of one accord and full of the Holy Ghost. It was an unusual presence of the power of God, a Pentecostal experience in my work for the Lord, that had never happened before.

As a lad I recall going to old-fashioned, shouting Methodist meetings with my mother and father. The congregation loved one another; they put their arms around one another, wept together, sang together, and rejoiced together. They had the "old-time religion."

I was called to conduct a meeting in a little town not far from my home. I had never been to the church where the meeting was to begin on Wednesday night and go through Sunday night. By Saturday night no decisions for Christ had been made. My heart was heavy. I remember going home Saturday night and praying that God would in some way speak in that little church during the last service.

On Sunday morning, a young man stood up to lead the singing, but he began to weep bitterly and was unable to sing. (His mother had died, and they had had her funeral in that church the day before.) I took the songbook and finished leading the song. After I had finished, I felt something come over me that I had never felt before in any other church service. There was a hush in the church, and I felt the presence of the Lord and the power of God.

I stood and asked, "How many of you people have ever heard the song "Take Your Burden to the Lord and Leave It There"? Many lifted their hands. I took the songbook and began singing, "If the world from you withhold of its silver and its gold. . . ." As I was singing, God began to speak to my heart; and after the second stanza, although I did not ask for an invitation, the people began to come forward and get on their knees to pray. I sang another stanza, and more people came forward. Before long, almost everyone in the church was down on their knees, praying.

I stopped singing, but the music played on. Heaven seemed to light the church; and the people began to sing, pray, shout, and weep as I had never seen. They were all of "one accord in one place," as we read in the book of Acts. An experience like that on the Day of Pentecost came upon us. I never preached at all that day. I would sing a little while and the people would come, weeping, rejoicing, and shouting. I immediately thought of 2 Chronicles 7. When the glory of the Lord filled the house, the priests could not enter into the house of the Lord. This truly was the Pentecostal experience I had prayed for.

It was not only an emotional event, but a revelation. Eighteen souls were saved that day! Every lost soul in the church was saved before the service was over! It was the presence of God, and I praised God all the way home.

When I got home, my wife looked at my face and said, "What in the world has happened to you?" I said, "Honey, sit down and let me tell you about it."

This has happened to me only once in a church service.

How I wish it would happen again! My prayer has been, "Do it again, Lord; do it again." "Not by might, nor by power, but by my spirit, saith the Lord" (Zech. 4:6).

The Golden Rule Religion

I was standing on a street corner one day, waiting for a traffic light to change, when a successful businessman approached and asked in a sarcastic tone, "Toles, are you still preaching?" My reply was that I desired to be faithful to the call of God in my life, and I hoped he was trusting in the Lord Jesus for his salvation and eternity.

"Toles," he said, "I live by the golden rule, and that's good enough for me." Quickly I replied, "The Golden Rule will do to live by, but it won't do to die by. When the death rattle comes in your throat, what really counts is what you did with Jesus." He resented that, laughed, and said, "You talk like a fool. Your religion is silly."

As we went our separate ways, I said, "I'm going to be praying for you, my friend." He made a smart remark as he walked away. Somehow I could not get him off my mind and heart. In less than a week, that man dropped dead with a heart attack on the same street where we had been talking.

I was shocked, remembering the incident, and felt constrained to pay my last respects by going to the funeral home. Looking down into the face of that man, I could not help saying to myself, "Brother, your soul is either with the Lord or in hell, without hope, without Christ." Standing there speechless for a moment, I thought about Jesus' parable of the rich fool. It became a living reality to my soul.

Men may laugh, scoff, and call you a fool; but remember that there is only one heartbeat between life and death. According to the Bible, the fool is the man who says there is no God.

During the many years of business life, I have dealt with men who feel that if they treat their fellowmen right and live by the Golden Rule, they have nothing to fear. Good works are noble things, but let us not forget the words of the apostle Paul, "For by grace are ye saved through faith; and that not of yourselves: it is the gift of God: Not of works, lest any man should boast" (Eph. 2:8-9).

"For with God Nothing Shall Be Impossible" (Luke 1:37)

Jesus carries out and fulfills all of God's promises, no matter how many of them there are. John Knox grasped all of Scotland in his strong faith, resting on the promises of God. John Wesley turned thousands of souls to the Lord because he believed the promises of God. Charles Finney's sermons shook a whole country and sent a wave of blessings through the churches because he believed nothing was impossible with God.

God sometimes uses sorrow in our lives to help us turn away from sin and seek eternal life. Every day we read of fine, cultured, educated people who have willingly or unwittingly become involved in unlawful activities. Often these things begin innocently, but they end tragically when people fail to realize the possible results of their actions.

Those people are shocked when hindsight, the sharpest and most cruel of all perspectives, reveals the stupidity of their poor judgment. There are people in our society whose disregard for law is a way of life and whose consciences are distorted to justify their actions. Unlike these hard-core lawbreakers, the man who has always thought of himself as an upright citizen is brought so low by conscience and grief of his misdeeds that he often allows self-persecution to destroy him; and those who love him can be equally destroyed by his distress.

Such was the case of a pharmacist who had been tried and convicted for selling illegal drugs. Unable to face the public or even his friends, he remained secluded in his home, awaiting the day he was to report to prison if the judge refused his appeal for a new trial. So unbearable was the burden that he called the pastor and asked him to come to the house. That very week I was conducting a layman-led crusade in the church near the pharmacist's home. The pastor asked me to accompany him to visit the man. Upon arrival, we were invited in and met his lovely wife and children.

He talked freely of his problems and his worries about the

future. I felt led to assure him that we had all made mistakes. No one is perfect except Jesus. Our Lord loves and cares, and he is concerned about our worries and is anxious to help if we are willing to confess our sins and ask for his help. God would make a new man of him. God made a promise. "Therefore if any man be in Christ, he is a new creature: old things are passed away; behold, all things are become new" (2 Cor. 5:17). He has given us both his promise and his oath, two things we can completely count on, for it is impossible for God to tell a lie.

We knelt together in prayer. He and his family accepted Christ as their Savior. Afterward, I explained that he must now proclaim his decision to the world by coming forth in the church to make public his confession of faith. This was a difficult thing to ask of a man who had for weeks refused to see anyone. However, he and his family were of one accord and quickly agreed that he would do so.

That evening when I gave the invitation at the church, they came forward. He turned to the congregation and said, "I'm ashamed of my life, what I've done to my family and my Lord; but he is not ashamed of me because he loves me. I'm going to serve my time in prison and be a soul-winner." True to his word and promise to God, he taught a Bible class in prison, won souls to Christ, and grew strong in his walk with the Lord.

Two years later, after his release from prison, he became a leader in the church and a dedicated soul-winner. My soul rejoiced when I returned for the second meeting in that same church two years later and found him a glowing example of a true Christian, forgetting the past, pressing forward to the future, realizing his past sins were forgiven and forgotten.

Several years ago I received a letter from him, rejoicing over answered prayer and praising God for the glorious victory found only in Jesus Christ. He said, "I learned the hard way. What God promises, he is able to do, for he did it for me."

What a wonderful God we have! He is the Father of our Lord Jesus Christ, the source of every mercy, and the one who so wonderfully comforts and strengthens us in our hardships and trials. Why does he do this? So that when others are troubled, needing our sympathy and encouragement, we can pass on to them that same help and comfort God has given us.

God Knows Best

"Righteous art thou, O Lord, and upright are thy judgments. Thy testimonies that thou hast commanded are righteous and very faithful" (Ps. 119:137-138).

Those who preach have their moments of weariness and despair, as do all Christians. We have our testings, trials, and daily decisions to make. Satan never lets up and never plays favorites.

My decision to accept an invitation to conduct a revival in South Carolina seemed to lack the usual enthusiasm. I reluctantly made the long trip and arrived at the East Coast city in the midst of a violent storm. The storm made it difficult to locate the church, which was three miles out of town. I stopped at a service station, seeking directions first to the church and then to the home where I was to stay during the week-long revival. Often, when conducting a meeting in a place I have never been, I first drive to the church, desiring to see the location—but more important, to be alone and pray for the meeting.

I drove to the church; and while waiting for the wind and rain to subside, I sat in my car, watching as the wind forced the front doors of the little church to swing back and forth. Evidently someone had forgotten to lock them. The fury of the storm and the desolation surrounding the small country church only added to my depression. The devil's temptation to abandon the call and return home was almost overwhelming. It took fervent prayer that afternoon to remain faithful to the Lord. I recall praying, "Lord, you've called me to do a job. I must obey, regardless of the circumstances."

Suddenly the Lord spoke to me: "I brought you here to do a job. I am with you." I felt the peace of God. When I arrived at the lovely home of the full-blooded Indian people, I was

E. B. Toles with his friend, Governor George Busbee of Georgia

E. B. and his wife, Mildred, in the House Chamber

Preaching in Grady Wilson's crusade in Alabama

E. B. is remembered by nationally famous political cartoonist, Baldy, of *The Atlanta Constitution.*

Being administered the oath of office

E. B. and Mildred on the right with the James Waters at left and evangelist Billy Graham, center—Jack P. Lowndes in the back

Mildred and E. B. with then Governor and Mrs. Jimmy Carter

Two long-time friends, E. B. and evangelist Grady Wilson of the Billy Graham team

received with a warm Christian welcome.

That church could seat about two hundred people. Before the week was over the pews and aisles were filled. God showered his blessings on the services, and many souls were saved. We never know what God has in store for us if we will be faithful and obedient! I am sure most of us have had occasions when it seemed hard to do what God wanted us to do. I have learned he has ways of teaching us lessons.

Perhaps my experience as a boy could best summarize it. I was raised on a farm, and I learned many great lessons from my father. One day while plowing in the field, my brother and I began to throw clods of dirt at the old mules to see which could get to the end of the row the quicker. Since my father was not present, we simply played at the job and took our hands from the plow. You can imagine what crooked rows we made. My father had taught us to always hold on to the plow and never look back in order to make a straight row. When he returned to the field, just one look was all that was necessary; and he took me to the woodshed! I trust you understand that he made an impression *in my life* and *on my life* with a razor strap, but thank the Lord for it! Jesus said, "No man, having put his hand to the plough, and looking back, is fit for the kingdom of God" (Luke 9:62).

It Would Have Been Wrong

Once, during a sermon, I referred to an incident that happened to me in the state of Illinois, where I was conducting a two-week revival. After one of the evening services, we stood about and talked at length. Consequently, it was quite late when I returned to my hotel. Not accustomed to the extreme, freezing temperatures outside and the intense heat inside, I felt very tired and thirsty.

Inquiring of the innkeeper where I could purchase a soft drink, I was directed to the hotel bar, the only concession open at that late hour. Without thinking, I headed in that direction and then realized that no matter how great my thirst, I could not justify, as a man preaching the Word of God, patronizing a bar. The thought occurred to me that if I went to the bar to get a soft drink, it would be a hypocrisy to all I had preached. Without hesitation I returned to my room and satisfied my thirst with water.

It seems incredible that ten years later I should mention such a small incident, since it was only a reflection and not a major point in my sermon. However, there was a man sitting in the audience who was in the liquor business. When the invitation was given, he came forward and got right with God. Soon he got out of the liquor business and eventually became successful in another business. He became active in that church and began to win souls to Jesus Christ. I have a letter in my file from him, saying, "God put that experience in your life just for me. Thank you."

No experience is too insignificant for the Lord to use in winning souls. We never know when we relate a true experience if it will convict someone of his wrongdoing.

Dwight L. Moody said that he had read of an old man who had gone to California to see his son, who had become rich. He traveled on a train all the way across the United States. Upon his arrival, his son asked him to go to a tavern. He replied, "I've traveled too far, but not far enough to forget my principles and convictions." If a man will not stand for something, he'll fall for anything. "Stand therefore, having your loins girt about with truth, and having on the breastplate of righteousness; And your feet shod with the preparation of the gospel of peace; Above all, taking the shield of faith, wherewith ye shall be able to quench all the fiery darts of the wicked. And take the helmet of salvation, and the sword of the Spirit, which is the word of God" (Eph. 6:14-17).

The great need for Christians today is to take their stand and to remain firm regardless of what the world may say. Martin Luther was asked about his firm stand and convictions: "If you continue your stand and hold to this way of life—where will you be?" He replied quickly, "I'll be where I've always been, in the hands of Almighty God."

8

No Deal

A wealthy man in Rome (now deceased) called to inform me of a possible return on a $50,000 investment. "Would you be interested?" he asked me. My reply was, "Yes, let's take a look at it tomorrow." We drove to the property, where he gave me the plans and blueprint for a building that was to be erected. After looking the deal over and giving it careful consideration, we had a verbal agreement. It was a deal, although I had not signed a contract. He said, "Your word is good enough for me, Mr. Toles."

During the night I awoke and God seemed to be saying something about the real estate deal, but I was not quite sure just what was wrong. Frankly, I could not sleep after being awakened, so I was convinced that I must go back to Mr. _____ to question him further. The next morning, I called and asked if I could see him at once.

As we drove out to look at the property again, words came to me out of a blue sky: "Do you know if this concern plans to sell alcoholic beverages in this place once it is completed and in operation?" His reply was honest. He did not know and had not given that a thought, but he assured me that we could find out with a phone call. He made the call and informed me, "Yes, they would stock alcoholic beverages in the store."

I looked him in the eye and said, "I gave you my word yesterday; verbally we made a deal, but *it is no deal.* You have known me for twenty-five years. I am a man of my word, but I want to tell you I learned something at my mother's knee that means more to me than all the money in the world. Money and investments are not that important. Sir, will you let me back out of this deal?" He took me by the hand and said, "Thank God for a man of convictions. I feel the same way you do; let's both forget the whole thing." This we did.

Some weeks later a beautiful letter came to me from that good man, expressing his gratitude and appreciation for the stand I took. I am sure I have read it a hundred times. He was a shrewd businessman, but he had deep religious principles and character. God honored him during his ninety-odd years of life, and I am told he left a substantial amount of money to his church.

Mr. Businessman, some things are more important in this life than good investments and money. Listen to the writer of Proverbs: "For wisdom is better than rubies; and all the things that may be desired are not to be compared to it" (Prov. 8:11).

Their Reward Shall Be Prosperity and Happiness

God does so much for us. We who put our faith and trust in him receive his blessings throughout life and into eternity. A dear friend, who had one of the sweetest Christian spirits of any man I have ever known, lived by the words "You can never outgive God." He gave generously of his business profits, believing it all belonged to God anyway and he was merely the administrator. He was starting out in business on a shoe-string. Sales were slow, and true profit was seemingly in the far distant future. Cheerfully he returned the Lord's portion of the profits before paying his business debts.

One day I said to him, "In ten years God's going to make you rich," With a smile on his face he replied, "I'm already rich—rich in the Lord." "Yes," I said, "but I mean financially. Let's take note of this conversation and a decade from now we'll take inventory. You love God and strive to please him in every way. Remember the psalmist's words, 'But his delight is in the law of the Lord; and in his law doth he meditate day and night. And he shall be like a tree planted by the rivers of water, that bringeth forth his fruit in his season; his leaf also shall not wither; and whatsoever he doeth shall prosper'" (Ps. 1:2-3).

His Christian life was devoted to winning souls to Christ. Each morning, long before daybreak, he would arise to begin the day with Bible study and fervent prayer. His love for Jesus overflowed and brought men flocking to his Sunday School class. He bubbled with joy and praise to God. Ten years passed. God had opened doors and brought opportunities he never dreamed would come. He had built a new place of business and a beautiful home.

One evening, I received a call from him. He reminded me of our conversation years before and invited my wife and me to share in the ceremony dedicating his new home and business to the Lord. Today he is a man of wealth, but he will quickly tell you, "It all belongs to God."

Our wonderful Lord is ever giving and never withdraws his hand from those who desire his best. Who has ever risen from his table unsatisfied or returned from his door unblessed? The apostle Paul had this to say: "Who giveth us richly all things to enjoy" (1 Tim. 6:17). I am reminded of a business acquaintance, who, when dealing in real estate, always insists that the proposition must be a bargain or he is not interested.

Perhaps many are looking for a shortcut with God or a spiritual bargain. My reader, there is no such thing as a spiritual bargain or a shortcut with God. It seems that we are living in an age when some people are looking for something for nothing. Let us never forget that somewhere, sometime, someone had to pay a price. When we really and truly fall in love with Jesus, we never ask, "What's in it for me?" but rather, "Lord, what wilt thou have me do?"

Trouble

"The Lord is good, a strong hold in the day of trouble; and he knoweth them that trust in him" (Nah. 1:7). Who of us has not had troubles? Life is not a bed of roses. Job so well said, "Man that is born of woman is of few days, and full of trouble" (Job 14:1). The important thing is how we cope with trouble. No matter the extent or term of our troubles, our deliverance is always answered by a healing of the mind, body, and soul. Many times we concentrate our prayers on relief of

immediate needs, but the Lord sees a much broader picture
of our needs.

A man of great means had a deformed eighteen-year-old
son who was confined to bed and required the attendance of
a full-time nurse. As that man and I sat beside the bed of his
frail young son, the father told me a story of joy. Everything
possible had been done in seeking help for the child. After
years of fruitless efforts, he and his wife had become weary;
and they had begun to look upon the child as a problem and
burden.

Finally, the parents placed everything in God's hands; the
son was not miraculously healed, but the husband and the wife
were "healed" in mind, body, and soul. They accepted Jesus
as the Master of their lives. The child was no longer a burden,
but a joy to them. Because of that afflicted son, they found
Jesus and reaped countless blessings that might never have
been theirs.

Jesus Christ loves you and wants to help with your troubles,
but *you* must come to *him*. You may not understand all the
messages God has for us, but rest assured that the Lord is
good and will never turn away anyone who seeks him. He
does not promise a life free from trouble or sorrow; nor does
he explain all the injustices of the world; however, his promise
of strength, love, mercy, and guidance is ours for the asking
and is never denied, as in the case of Hezekiah.

Hezekiah had great problems and was deathly ill (2 Kings
20). A prophet of God came and told him to "Set thine house
in order; for thou shalt die" (v. 1). Hezekiah turned his face
to the wall and began to pray. God heard his prayer and looked
into his heart and saw his goodness. He healed his body and
added fifteen years to his life! So, my friend, when trouble
comes, turn to God.

The unsaved do not have that stronghold in the day of trouble
if they do not know Christ as Savior. "But the wicked are like
the troubled sea, when it cannot rest, whose water cast up
mire and dirt" (Isa. 57:20).

Psalm 77:1-13 tells of a man in trouble; not only was he

troubled, but sick. (Note v. 10.) Here we find the psalmist crying to God. He was so troubled that he could not sleep (v. 4) and even questioned God's promise (vv. 7-9). We note that he said in verses 11-12: "I will remember the works of the Lord: surely I will remember thy wonders of old. I will meditate also of all thy work, and talk of thy doings." Truly the psalmist knew many troubles, but he held to God in spite of them all.

Trouble usually results in one of two things: It will either bring you closer to God or turn you further from him. Some years ago, I was visiting a hospital with a friend whose son was dying of cancer. The father was a multimillionaire. He told the doctors he did not care what the cost was. If it took a million dollars, he wanted to send his son to any other doctor or hospital in the world. He just wanted his son to live; but, regretfully, the son died. The words of the doctors still ring in my ears: "Sir, there are some things money cannot buy— money cannot buy life; that's in the hands of God."

We have heard all our lives that "money talks." Perhaps sometimes it does, but it does not always give us the right answer.

Life's goal should not simply be to get rich, but rather to enrich the world around us. A brilliant man had this to say about the subject: "What availeth it if we become so engrossed in the pursuit of business or of money for its own sake, after we've earned an adequate amount, if this pursuit unfits us for the enjoyment of the real, true, deep, satisfying things of life; if it blinds our eyes, warps our souls, and numbs our better senses and sensibilities, then money will never bring happiness, but many times troubles and, perhaps, problems we've never anticipated."

He Said, "I Don't Believe"

In the early days of our business, before we hired men to go out and collect on accounts, we had to make the weekly collections. It was nearing dusk one Saturday as I made my last call. Each week at a particular house there were the smell of alcohol, noise or people in the kitchen, and the rattle of

drinking glasses as whiskey was poured. The owner was a bootlegger who sold whiskey by the drink.

Many times I had witnessed to him but my words fell on
deaf ears. He was a wicked man. He cursed God and said he
did not believe in God or the Bible; and he claimed that heaven
and hell were sheer nonsense. His wife attended church upon
occasion and did not approve of his activities. She appreciated
my efforts to win him to the Lord.

On that particular Saturday, after I entered his house a violent storm broke. Because of the hazardous driving conditions,
I could not leave and decided that was a perfect time to discuss
the Bible with him and give testimony of the Lord Jesus Christ
and what he meant to me.

It has always been my conviction to choose Scriptures which
are appropriate to the person with whom I am talking. I said,
"Mr. _____, you know you are getting old. Your three-score
years and ten have passed; and, at best, you don't have many
years left. You need to give serious thought to the matter of
where you are going to spend eternity." He laughed, made
fun of me, and said, "Toles, I don't believe in this God business.
There is nothing to it. We are all just like dogs when we die—
that is the last of us." "Now surely you don't believe that," I
replied. "The Scripture teaches us that God breathed the
breath of life into man's nostrils and he became a living soul
and that soul is going to spend eternity somewhere, either in
heaven or in hell. He laughed and said, "There is no such
thing as hell. You have your hell here on earth."

The conversation went on for several minutes; it was almost
dark. Lightning flashed across the sky and seemed to light up
the room. I said to him, "Do you hear the roar of that thunder
and see that flash of lightning? This is God. Only God can do
that." "Why, Toles, I don't believe in that God. That's your
God, not my God."

"Man, surely you don't mean to tell me that you are an
atheist and that you don't believe in God. Sir, the day will
come when you will call on God." He laughed again, walked
to the front door, and, pushing the door open, rolled up his

sleeve, doubled up his fist, and cursed God! He said, "If there be a God, strike me dead."

"Man, don't do that!" I exclaimed. "You are tempting God. You are shaking your fist in the face of the living God!" I felt as if I must get out of the presence of that wicked man. Looking him straight in the eye, I said, "The day will come when you will call on God."

The downpour slackened. Thanking God for safety, I went my way. In less than three weeks I received a telephone call from his wife, asking me to come quickly to the hospital. Upon arrival, I found him gasping for breath. Looking into his face and remembering his words, I knew that here was a man literally hellbound! He had tempted God and cursed him. He had laughed in the face of God!

I began to tell him about Jesus. He knew death was only a heartbeat away: hell and eternity. As I quoted Scripture, the man reached out, took my hand, and called upon God for mercy and forgiveness. He was saved! The doctors said he would not live, but he did. I gave him a Gideon New Testament and underscored John 3:16, Romans 10:9-10, and Ephesians 2:8, telling him to memorize them. He stayed in the hospital about eight weeks and then went back to his home—but not to sell whiskey.

He sold the home and moved to a different part of the country. I can see him now as he sat in a big rocking chair on the porch, with the Testament in his hand. On each trip I made to his home after his conversion, though he could hardly speak above a whisper, he said, "Toles, I got in, I got in!"

That man was never able to go to church, but he lived about two years after being stricken by illness. His wife and sons and other members of his family became Christians because of what they had seen happen in his life. As I think back, I believe that was one of the greatest conversions I can remember. Thank God, he found his way.

That, to me, is one of the experiences that proves that God is no respecter of persons and that Jesus Christ is still in the soul-saving business. The hardest sinner had called upon God, and the Lord heard him. That's what I call power: the power of God to save a wicked man. "For the word of God is quick, and powerful, and sharper than any two-edged sword, piercing even to the dividing asunder of soul and spirit, and of the joints and marrow, and is a discerner of the thoughts and intents of the heart" (Heb. 4:12).

Yes, truly the word of God is powerful and *sharp;* it is sharper than a sword; it cuts deep; it will cause a wicked, cursing bootlegger to call upon God and turn to his Son, Jesus Christ, for salvation.

God said, "Behold, I am the Lord, the God of all flesh: is there any thing too hard for me?" (Jer. 32:27).

Deacon Prayer Retreat

"This is a true saying, if a man desire the office of a bishop, he desireth a good work" (1 Tim. 3:1).

It was a joy and an honor to be invited to lead a deacons' prayer retreat at a friend's lakeside resort. The setting was tranquil and picturesque among the large oaks adorned with Spanish moss that gently swayed with the slightest breeze.

It had been my pleasure some months before to stay with a dedicated Christian family while conducting a week's revival service. Many souls were saved in the meeting, and it was with great anticipation that I looked forward to going back to that town and renewing the acquaintances and friendships I had made during the revival.

Each night of the retreat, we had about fifty deacons in attendance. We shared experiences, discussed Scripture, and prayed together. The last evening was an unforgettable experience. While we were on our knees praying, one of the deacons stood and with great emotion exclaimed, "Men, I'm lost; I've been a hypocrite all my life. There is sin in my life, sin I've hidden from man and tried to hide from God." He continued by confessing his sins and asking God's forgiveness. We joined with him in praising God for removing this burden and for his wonderful gift of rebirth.

Others began to confess their sins and rededicate their lives to the Lord. The Holy Spirit's presence was strong within that group, and we continued to pray and rejoice in the Lord until the early hours of the morning. The Lord used that deacon to bring others closer to him. By rededicating his life he was relieved of his burden of sin; and he was able to witness, in truth and with conviction, to countless others.

In 1 Timothy Paul plainly told us the kind of men God wants as pastors and deacons to lead his people. The summation and effect of these qualities are: Let them follow the way you teach and live; be a pattern for them in your love, your faith, and your clean thoughts. It is true that the way to live a godly life is not an easy matter. Stay true to what is right, and God will bless you and use you to help others.

9

Too Late

Procrastination is one of the devil's most forceful tools. The twenty-fourth chapter of Acts tells how Paul stood before Felix, and Paul witnessed to him of the saving knowledge of Jesus Christ. "After certain days, when Felix came with his wife, Drusilla, which was a Jewess, he sent for Paul, and heard him concerning the faith in Christ. And as he reasoned of righteousness, temperance, and judgment to come, Felix trembled, and answered, Go thy way for this time; and when I have a convenient season, I will call for thee" (vv. 24-25). Felix trembled at the gospel. Paul gave him God's simple message: "Prepare to meet thy God," but Felix was waiting for a more convenient season.

An experience of a few years past gives another illustration of the consequences of procrastination. A businessman whom I had done business with and had witnessed to came down with a terminal illness. He was not aware of the seriousness of his condition when he entered the hospital. He was operated on and the doctor's diagnosis was "a very short time to live, perhaps a few weeks."

That man had not darkened the church door in ten years. Soon after his operation, he asked his wife to call and ask me to come to the hospital to see him. He had been a friend of mine for many years. That evening after work, as I drove to the hospital, I had a strange feeling about that man; and my heart was saddened with compassion because his wife had informed me that he did not know the seriousness of his illness. As I entered the door of his hospital room, he asked me to pray for him. He said, "E. B., when I get well, I'm going back

97

to my church; I haven't been there in ten years, but I'm going to walk down the aisle to the front, take the preacher by the hand, and dedicate the remainder of my years to living a Christian life."

He had waited too late. This is true, so true, with many people. They wait until tragedy strikes or death is upon them, and then they begin to try to straighten out their lives. This was true in the life of that man. He assured me he was a Christian and was saved when he was a young man, but he became so busy in his business and so involved in his own affairs that he did not have time for God. He was just too late to live the Christian life he now desired. Many men whom I have known through the years have put their business between them, their Lord, and their church. I, too, was guilty of that very thing. It was one of the great sins in my life before surrendering completely to the Lord. Anyone who gets involved in his own business, with little or no time for God, is simply too busy!

We talked of Scripture and prayed. He asked if I would come back to see him again, and I promised to come back. Because he was dying, he was in my prayers and on my heart and mind constantly. During my second visit to the hospital, the Lord gave me the words and opened the way to approach him. Realizing his days were short on this earth, I discussed the love of God and his mercy toward us. After we prayed and read some Scripture, I noticed that his body and the tone of his voice appeared weaker; but again he repeated his desire to rededicate his life to the Lord. As I stood beside his bed, holding his hand, I thought, *Oh, my friend, you don't know that when you go back to the church, you'll be in your casket.*

He said to me, "I have failed God." Those words have made a great impression on my life. That was a grim reminder that I too failed God, but how I thanked God that I was not like the man who was dying and unaware of death's rapid approach.

He had asked me to come back the fourth time. As I entered his room, I was well aware that this would be my last time to see and speak to him. I read a few verses of Scripture and prayed with him. His voice was only a whisper; I leaned closer to hear his words as he said, "When I get well I'm going back to my church." That was all he could say. Tears rolled down my cheeks as I thought, "E. B., only but by the grace of God, this could be you." Leaving the room, I pondered on what he said; and oh, how mindful I was that I needed to be more faithful to my Lord!

How many people like that friend of mine have failed in their opportunity to serve God by waiting for a more convenient time? Are you putting off God's plan of salvation? Perhaps some who read these lines have never come to face the fact that life is short. Someone said, "The wood in the cradle touches the marble in the tomb." As we think of eternity compared with this short life, it behooves us to always be prepared to meet God.

On leaving the hospital that day, I knew I would not see my friend alive again. The next day he died. His words kept ringing in my ears; and as they rolled the casket down the aisle of the church, it seemed as though I heard him saying, "When I get well, I'm going back to church, walk down the aisle, and take the preacher by the hand." Yes, it was too late.

Do not put off until tomorrow what needs to be done for God today. No one has the assurance that he will be alive tomorrow. David in 1 Samuel 20:3 said, "There is but a step between me and death." Also Solomon, the wisest man who ever lived, said in Proverbs 27:1, "Boast not thyself of tomorrow; for thou knowest not what a day may bring forth."

Learning to Live

It was midnight when I received a call from a registered nurse who had heard me preach a sermon on hell. She said, "Mr. Toles, even though I work at the hospital and see many people die, hell had never made much of an impression on me until I began thinking about my own life and how I was not prepared to meet God and was bound for hell. I tried to get it out of my mind but I couldn't. As weeks went by after hearing you preach, every time someone passed away, your message on hell and the story about the rich man in hell, lifting up his eyes in torment, rang in my ears. I'm well aware that some people do not believe in hell; but I do, and I need help. I'm smoking one cigarette after another, taking tranquilizers, and I can't relax. Something has to be done. I'm miserable; I'm going to hell." We had prayer on the phone. I asked her to read some Scripture and made an appointment to meet with her the next morning. In a quiet corner of my store, we talked; and she told me much about her life.

As I was reading some Scripture to her, she said, "Stop, please wait—you need not read any more; I'm here to have you tell me how to become a Christian." Immediately I gave her some simple Scriptures: John 3:16, Romans 10:9-10, and Ephesians 2:8, and assured her that Jesus said, "Him that cometh to me I will in no wise cast out" (John 6:37). One has to come to ask Jesus to save him. We got on our knees, and she confessed Christ as Lord and Savior and was gloriously saved.

That woman went about her daily routine in the hospital, living a happy Christian life. I checked on her several months later and found that she was still rejoicing in the Lord.

We never know when we preach or speak who might be listening or what might be said that will touch a heart. Even though that woman had to ponder my sermon for several months, the seed was planted; the Holy Spirit did the work; and she finally was convinced to make a decision for Christ.

Is there a sweeter word in any language than "forgiveness," when it sounds in a sinner's ear like the silver notes of jubilee to the captive Israelite? What riches of grace does free forgiveness exhibit? To forgive fully, freely, forever! Here is a consultation of wonder and a miracle. This is the precious thing about forgiveness in the name of the Lord, as it was with the nurse when she found Christ Jesus as her Lord.

We must all die. But thanks be unto God for his love toward us, that by accepting Jesus Christ as our Lord and Savior as did the nurse, we need not fear death and hell. God's Word tells us in simple language the way to heaven, but let us never forget that there is a place called hell, and it is real. "And in hell he lift up his eyes, being in torments, and seeth Abraham afar off, and Lazarus in his bosom" (Luke 16:23).

Nothing Between

In July 1933, many people mourned the passing of Dr. Charles A. Tindley, a great hymn writer and onetime slave, who dedicated his life to God and humanity. A theologian asked one of Dr. Tindley's twelve children, "How did your father achieve so many great accomplishments? The youth replied, "On his knees."

While visiting in my home, Dr. Charles F. Weigle, also a songwriter, told me about the first time he heard Dr. Tindley sing the hymn "Nothing Between" to a congregation. There had been no sermon and no invitation given, but hundreds of people came forward accepting Christ and rededicating their lives as he continued to sing.

Let us ask ourselves, "What's between God and me? Is my life in tune and in touch with God?" When there is nothing between you and God, you have a direct line to heaven, a communication that is free to all. In one of John Wesley's sermons, he prayed, "Sink me, O God, to perfection's height." Never in the history of man has the need been greater for man to put himself at God's disposal. None of us is indispensable. Everyone is important and has a solemn obligation to give his best to God and man. Jesus said, "Follow me, and I will make you fishers of men" (Matt. 4:19).

Fame is generally given to the dead; wealth is obtained by the few; but happiness is the greatest boon of all. And truly lasting happiness can be found only through Jesus Christ. Dr. George W. Truett said, "To seek God's will is the greatest gift . . . to know God's will is the greatest knowledge . . . to do God's will is the greatest privilege."

Several references have been made in this book to my deacon friend who had a boundless eagerness to serve the Lord. As he so aptly prayed, "Lord, we came up on the rough side of the mountain and when it's time for me to go home to heaven, I want to get there draggin' tired!"

While I was conducting a layman-led meeting in a large southern city, the pastor asked me to visit a businessman who had been active in the church. Because of growing demands and prosperity as a certified public accountant, he had put Christ in the background of his life. He readily admitted he was not prepared to meet God even though he had been saved. I reminded him that it was God's gift that allowed him the ability to prosper. God would not want his gift to cause priorities, values, and responsibilities to be distorted.

One evening he and his family attended the worship service. I felt led to sing "Nothing Between" and after the song I asked the congregation to search their souls: "Is there *anything* between you and God?" Many hands were raised, and people began to come forward desiring prayer.

The businessman quickly came forward and stood before the congregation, telling how he had allowed so many things to come between himself and God that there was no longer any room for his Savior. As his wife and family came to his side, he confessed his sins and praised God, saying, "I'm tired of sin; I'm turning everything over to my Lord." This was a great victory for God. It was a blessed revival!

Windows of Heaven Opened

In a large southern city, I was conducting a week's meeting in one of the great old established churches that had a beautiful sanctuary and stained-glass windows. Near midweek I had an appointment for lunch with the pastor. As I walked through that beautiful structure on my way to the pastor's study, I passed by a young man washing windows. I said, "Young friend, you've got quite a job washing all these large windows." "Yes, sir," he replied. "I enjoy doing it, especially for the church. This is my kind of work."

I recalled the Scripture about Daniel as he opened his windows toward Jerusalem and knelt down to pray. In the book of Daniel, the decree of Darius was given after he signed the order that Daniel would be cast into the lion's den. In the sixth chapter, tenth verse, are these words: "Now when Daniel knew that the writing was signed, he went into his house; and his windows being open in his chamber toward Jerusalem, he kneeled upon his knees three times a day, and prayed, and gave thanks before his God, as he did aforetime." But even though Daniel was cast into the den of lions, he was untouchable because he was God's man.

After I had said a few words to him, he said, "Oh, you're the visiting preacher here, aren't you?" I said, "No, I'm the visiting speaker, but I'm not a preacher. You know, young man, I'm just ordinary like you; but I am conducting the meeting." That opened the door to witness to him, and I asked, "Are you a Christian?" With a quick reply he said, "No, sir."

I gave him a special invitation to be my honored guest that night. "Oh, no, sir; you see, I'm just a window washer, and I'd be out of place in this beautiful church. I don't even have clothes that would be fit to wear." Then I told him that Jesus loved the common man. As a matter of fact, the Bible makes reference many times to the laborer as well as to the rich man. Our conversation continued, but he became concerned that he would lose his job if he did not return to his window washing. I told him not to worry about that. Taking my New Testament, I began reading from Luke 10:30-37, the parable of the good Samaritan. I told him of the three people who passed by the poor man lying by the side of the road, needing help. No one except the good Samaritan paid him any attention. I asked him to read John 3:16 and then inquired if he believed what he had just read. "Well, I guess I do," he said. "That's what the Bible said, isn't it?" I asked if he believed Jesus loved him enough to die on a cross to save him and give him a home in heaven for eternity. A quick reply came back, "Yes, I do. I sure want to go to heaven when I die." We continued to talk and I gave him other Scripture to read.

There was a hunger in his soul, and even his countenance revealed a deep longing for the truth. Perhaps no one had really taken time to explain the Scripture to him in a simple manner. Here was a man washing windows in a church; yet he was lost and needed Christ.

We began to pray, and in his own humble way he asked the Lord Jesus to save him and to come into his heart. I asked if he would go with me to the pastor's study to tell him what happened. He asked, "Do you think I'll get fired?" I said, "I'll see to it that you are not fired."

We walked into the pastor's study, and I said, "Pastor, this young man was downstairs washing windows. He has something to tell you." He told the pastor what had happened to his life, and we joined in rejoicing with him. I told him that if he really meant business, he would come to church that night; but he declined, saying he would not be accepted without the proper clothes to wear. The pastor assured him he would.

I asked the pastor to postpone our luncheon date for another hour and took the young man to my hotel room, where I selected a nice suit of clothes to give him. He was grateful beyond words. "Now," I said, "Let's go home and tell your wife what's happened." He told his wife what had happened; and she, too, accepted Christ.

That night he and his wife were in church. My heart leaped with joy. That man kept his eyes focused on me all during the sermon. It was a glorious and happy occasion to be preaching, knowing that that man, who had just accepted Christ, was waiting for the invitation so he and his wife could come forward to make their profession of faith known. When the invitation was given they came forward, and he related his experience of the afternoon. This man's experience was the beginning of a revival in that church! The young man developed into a fine Christian and soul-winner. About a year later I inquired and was told he had been baptized, had joined the church, and was working for the Lord.

On a return engagement to that church I met him again. He was well dressed, had a better job, and was very active in the church. He told me he thanked God I had found him that day washing the church windows. "That changed my life and eternity. Now my family and I are happy serving the Lord."

Let us never forget that, as Christians, we are Jesus' spokesmen and mouthpieces. Christians need to become involved in soul-winning, witnessing, and using every opportunity when God opens a door. We never know if a person is just waiting for us to introduce him to Jesus. That was true in the case of the window washer, and I thank God he put that young man in my pathway.

Giving God Control

During the recession days of the early 1970s, with business failures, bankruptcy, and a general economic slump, many businessmen became despondent and disillusioned. Through the years experience has taught me that we must look to God in good times as well as bad times.

At the height of the business slump, a good friend was faced with some difficult business and personal problems that began to affect his health. He was a devout Christian, deacon, and teacher of God's word. He came to me, asking if we could talk and pray together. He was scheduled to speak at a church meeting that evening; but because of a migraine headache and a depression that had forced him to remain in bed for more than a week, he was weak and unable to go about the Lord's business. My first impulse was to turn to the Bible to quote a favorite Scripture, but the Holy Spirit spoke to me to merely give him chapters and verses to read at home.

I shared my experience of being a victim of migraine headaches for years and my search for medical relief. He seemed to gain solace from our conversation, and I could feel the presence of the Lord with me as we talked. I suggested that he cancel his engagement to speak. "Remember," I said, "God expects us to use common sense concerning our health and bodies. Go home! get in bed; and confess your faithfulness to God and your great desire to serve him! Ask for his healing hand to be laid upon your body and claim his promises. Then thank God and turn it all over to him."

On Sunday morning, when the invitation was given, that man rushed down the aisle and asked if he could speak to the congregation. To the best of my recollection, these are his words: "Friends, I want to tell what happened to me this week. Great problems had resulted in an illness I could not cope with; nor could I find relief. God led me to a layman in Rome, who gave me a plan to follow and Scripture to study. After following his advice, I felt the presence and power of God in my body, physically and spiritually. Folks, I've had a Pentecostal experience."

His moving story caused a hush to fall over the congregation. Then people began to come forward, rejoicing, and embracing one another and glorifying God. A spirit of revival filled the hearts and souls of the congregation.

The following week he came to my office and related the wonderful things that had taken place in his life since our last meeting. His headache had not returned, and his business was showing signs of becoming stable, with prospects of new growth. We praised God and gave all the glory to him. I told him not to let the fire go out but to keep God's flame burning brightly for all to see. The glow has not dimmed: The entire church and community continue to feel the impact of one man giving complete control of his life to God.

"Now thanks be unto God, which always causeth us to triumph in Christ, and maketh manifest the savour of his knowledge by us in every place" (2 Cor. 2:14).

10
Sowing the Seed

The Entertainer

A man entered our store one day and began to browse. Not knowing the man, I began to chat and asked what business he was in. "I'm in the greatest business in the world," came the reply. I put forth my hand and exclaimed, "Is that right? That's great! I'm in the same business. Yes, sir, it's the greatest in the world, God's business—winning people to the Lord." "You misunderstand," he corrected, "I'm in show business." I welcomed him to the city and told him it was a great place to meet Jesus if he did not already know him.

It took only a moment or two for him to decide he had come to the wrong place to pass the time. As he quickly turned to leave he asked, but did not wait for an answer, "Do you preach to all your customers?"

We boldly say what we believe just as the apostle Paul did when he said, "We also believe, and therefore speak." (2 Cor. 4:13).

Get Out of My Yard

A woman invited the pastor and me to visit her home to witness to her husband. We found him relaxing in the backyard. He greeted us by saying, "Preacher, what are you doing here?" We explained that we wanted to invite him to church. Even though his manner and tone of voice were anything but receptive, we continued to witness to him. It was evident that resentment and anger were building up in him.

Finally he stood up; and with a voice to match his formidable six-foot, two-hundred-pound frame, he told us, "I'm not inter-

ested in hearing anyone preach. Furthermore, I don't need
your love or God's love. You get out of here before I throw
you out."

As we left the yard, I told him we would be praying for
him. "Marvel not, my brethren, if the world hate you" (1 John
3:13).

Sunday . . . No Sale

"But the seventh day is the sabbath of the Lord thy God"
(Ex. 20:10).

An acquaintance of mine had just moved into the new home
he had built; and in honor of the occasion, he had planned
to entertain friends and relatives. He was a good customer,
and through the years he had purchased most of his furniture
from our store. He was not a Christian, but he knew I was
and also knew we operated our business on Christian principles.

Late Saturday afternoon, the day before his party, he and
his wife came to the store and selected a very elegant and
costly dining room suite. Business had been slack that week;
and when he started counting out hundred-dollar bills, saying
he wanted to pay cash, I was elated. Cash sales were a rarity
in those days. As the transaction was being completed, he told
me about the social gathering they had planned for Sunday
and said, "Toles, I'll need this delivered today." I explained
that our help had left for the day and it could not be delivered
until Monday.

"Well, all right," he said, "we'll just wait until tomorrow.
You can call the boys tonight and make arrangements to bring
it out to my house by ten o'clock tomorrow morning." Putting
my hand on his shoulder, I said, "Tomorrow is the Lord's Day,
and we have made it a practice never to work on Sunday."

"Oh," he replied, "It's not that important, Toles. The important thing for me is to get the furniture delivered. The most
important thing for you is that you have my money; and if
you want my business, you had better deliver that dining room
suite tomorrow!" "I certainly do want your business," I said,
"and I need the cash; but there is just no way I can deliver

this dining room suite tomorrow; I'll be in church."

He was beginning to get a little angry. "I want to ask you a question: Are you a big enough fool to stand there and tell me you would not deliver that furniture just because it is Sunday?"

"That's right," I said.

"You mean to tell me then you don't want my business?"

"I didn't say that," I replied. "I do want your business, but I don't want your business enough to deliver that dining room suite on the Lord's Day."

By this time he was red in the face with anger. He asked me to return his money and said, "You will never get another dime's worth of business from me! Any man who is that big a fool doesn't deserve my business."

I do not mind telling you that as badly as we needed the cash, it was mighty hard to return the money. Handing it to him, I assured him I regretted the incident. He walked out and never returned to our place of business. I do not know what kind of impression the matter made on his life, but I do know one thing: It did something for my brothers and me. We discussed it after he left and did not have any problem determining that I had done the right thing. We agreed that God would somehow send us more business to replace it. Surely enough, on Monday morning, soon after we opened the doors, a customer came in and bought not only the dining room suite the other man had selected, but also bought a living room suite, paying cash. Some may say this was a coincidence, but to us there was no doubt that the Lord had rewarded our refusal to yield to temptation with a sale amounting to more than double the original one, and paid for in cash!

"Blessed is the man that doeth this, and the son of man that layeth hold on it; that keepeth the sabbath from polluting it, and keepeth his hand from doing any evil" (Isa. 56:2).

Come Outside

One afternoon two men entered our place of business. One of the fellows had an account with us, which was several months in arrears. I called him aside and asked if he could make some arrangements to work toward settling the account.

It became immediately apparent that Slim was not completely sober, and the mention of his debt made him angry. With a torrent of curses and taking God's name in vain, he asked me to step outside and settle it by fighting; then he went further by saying he would cut my throat! It was obvious that the man did not realize the severity of his threats, but he assured me that he knew exactly what he was saying. I reached over the counter and put my hand on his shoulder. Red-faced with anger, he knocked my hand off and shouted obscenities to me.

"Slim, I don't want to fight; I've never found fighting to be a solution to anything; and besides," I laughed, "it takes too long to heal bones when you get to be my age." His mood and determination did not change. I offered to pray with him, which only brought more cursing. I let him know he would be on my prayer list, to allow Jesus to come into his life. With that, he stamped out of the store.

Not long after that, I saw Slim again. He was very kind and a gentleman in every respect. "Slim," I asked, "Do you remember the incident at the furniture store?" "Yes," he replied, "and I regret that."

I told him I was praying for him. This time he thanked me. We will never know how many people prayed for him or how many seeds had to be sown; but, thank God, they took time and did not judge him as a lost cause. Two years later I learned that Slim had accepted Jesus Christ and was attending church regularly. By coincidence, the pastor of the church had recently resigned, and several times they called upon me to speak.

One Sunday morning I saw Slim in the congregation, and my thoughts returned to the long road he had traveled since the day he had been so enraged and wanted to fight. "Slim," I said, "come up here; I want you to lead us in prayer for this church and for God's blessings on us today." He came forward and recalled in a whisper the day years before when he had cursed me.

Facing the congregation, he smiled and said, "Only God could work such a miracle. I love and appreciate this man. He has been a blessing to my life." The congregation did not understand what he was referring to, but it made my heart rejoice.

After the prayer I was ready to preach that morning, remembering the wise words of Solomon in Proverbs 18:19: "A brother offended is harder to be won than a strong city: and their contentions are like the bars of a castle."

Cart Before the Horse

For some years I taught a men's Bible class in my church. I invited a friend of mine, who was on the county police force, to attend. Soon he began coming to the class. After several Sundays I sensed in him a great hunger for the Lord. I told him on one occasion that I was praying for him, and I invited him to attend the revival services that were scheduled to begin very soon.

When I witnessed to my friend about the Lord, he said, "You know something, E. B.? I have a bad temper. The worst habit I have is cursing, and I don't believe a man who would do that is a Christian or should be a church member." I tried to explain to him that he had the cart before the horse; and related my experience as a boy, when I used bad language to my friend for pushing me in the creek. "A good man out of the good treasure of his heart bringeth forth that which is good; and an evil man out of the evil treasure of his heart bringeth forth that which is evil: for of the abundance of the heart his mouth speaketh" (Luke 6:45). I explained how Jesus could give him a new heart and could also help control his tongue. That was hard for him to understand, but after several days of meeting together and referring to Scripture, he was finally won to the Lord.

A short time later he revealed joyously that he had not had one bit of trouble controlling his cursing. "It just left me; I don't want to curse or use God's name in vain any more. I love Jesus now and want to live for him." I assured him that

that was evidence of his acceptance of Christ, and God would deliver him from the habit just as other men were delivered from other problems.

He became a dedicated Christian and was a true witness to many who felt, as he, that one must first cleanse himself of sin before accepting Christ. "Therefore being justified by faith, we have peace with God through our Lord Jesus Christ" (Rom. 5:1).

Covered Sin

The word of God, in Proverbs 28:13, says, "He that covereth his sins shall not prosper: but whoso confesseth and forsaketh them shall have mercy." Covered sin must be confessed. Sin hinders prayer; and when one has covered his sin, he cannot pray to God because he is not in the right relationship with the Lord. We are told in 1 John 1:9, "If we confess our sins, he is faithful and just to forgive us our sins."

Sin is the great destroyer, it wastes wealth; it wears away the human body, blights the intellect, withers the moral nature, weakens the will, deadens the conscience, hardens the heart, disgraces the life, and damns the soul.

That was so true in the life of a man who called my office and said he must see me immediately. We drove out of the city and up into the mountains. While we were driving very little was said. He seemed choked with tears. After we stopped, he told me he had been walking the floor at night and could not sleep. He was fearful of death because the doctors had told him that with his heart ailment he should avoid worrying. The man was desperate and his whole countenance revealed the depth of sorrow for his sins. He was a Sunday School teacher and a deacon. His whole family life was built around the church and Christian living. Yet he was living a liar's life, unfaithful to his wife.

He said, "Mr. Toles, what am I going to do? I'm a miserable wretch, living in hell. The doctors have warned me I have a serious heart ailment. I'm afraid to go to sleep for fear I'll not awake before I confess this sin and receive forgiveness."

I said, "Sir, let's get out of the car, get on our knees, and talk to God." He poured out his heart to God, confessing his sin. His prayer was like that of the psalmist of old: "Wash me and purge me, cleanse me, have mercy upon me, God, according to thy loving kindness, wash me thoroughly of my iniquity and cleanse me of my sins for I acknowledge my transgressions and my sin is ever before me. Create in me a clean heart." Within a year he had another serious heart attack and died, but the peace in his heart had brought joy and serenity to him and his family. Fortunately, he had discovered that man cannot be true to God or anyone else while covered sin fills the soul.

We should beware of light thoughts of sin. Thoughts kindle desires; desires lead to action; actions form habits; and habits repeated build character. All of it has to do with us in this mortal life and the life to come. Vicious imaginations and evil thoughts are the kindling wood that builds the fires of passionate desires; therefore, we should guard our thoughts. By degrees man becomes familiar with sin. We throw a cloak over it. We call it by dainty names.

Let us never forget that sin has a payday: Be sure your sin will find you out. If there is covered sin in your life, confess and forsake it. Cling to the old rugged cross.

Fruit Gatherers

Jesus said, "Ye have not chosen me, but I have chosen you, and ordained you, that ye should go and bring forth fruit, and that your fruit should remain: that whatsoever ye shall ask of the Father in my name, he may give it you" (John 15:16). And Paul said in Romans 7:4, "We should bring forth fruit unto God."

I was invited to participate in crusades in the states of Washington, Oregon, California, and Nevada. It was harvesttime; and the trees with their ripened fruit were arrayed in colorful splendor. In Oregon the pastor of the church where I was preaching said a man who was seriously ill had requested that I come visit him. We drove through the beautiful countryside to his home, nestled amidst orchards of cherry trees and other fruit trees. Here I found a Christian man with a smile on his face, not bitter that he was soon to leave his earthly home, but a praying, smiling saint of God.

He said, "Sir, I asked the preacher to have you come because I wanted to thank you for coming this distance to preach in our church and also to share with you a little bit of my own life's experiences." That day was a blessing to my life, and many of my sermon topics have come from our conversation that day. After we had prayed together, he asked his wife to take me out to see the vineyard and especially to see the cherry trees. They were beautiful, and the branches were heavy with big red cherries. I gathered a sackful.

When we returned to the house the man, confident of the beauty I had beheld, asked what I thought about the cherry trees. I assured him that they were beautiful and the fruit was delicious. I said to him, "You know, I'm a small business-man, not an ordained minister—just a fruit gatherer like your-self." A sweet smile came across his face as he said, "I've been a fruit gatherer all my life, not only gathering fruit in my vine-yard, but witnessing for the Lord and having the privilege of winning people to Jesus."

I said, "You know, Jesus called me not to be a pastor, but to be a fruit gatherer. I've been all over the country plucking fruit here and there for my Lord. Sometimes I find some that are not as ripe as those red cherries, and sometimes there are those that have already fallen to the ground and decayed. You have to work hard. Sometimes you win them and some-times you don't."

Too soon, it was time to leave that wonderful Christian. I assured him that if we did not meet again on this earth, we would surely meet in heaven. We clasped hands, and he quoted John 4:35-36: "Say not ye, There are yet four months, and then cometh harvest? behold, I say unto you, Lift up your eyes, and look on the fields; for they are white already to har-vest. And he that reapeth receiveth wages, and gathereth fruit unto life eternal: that both he that soweth and he that reapeth may rejoice together."

It is a blessed event which will occur to all believers in God's own time—the going home to be with Jesus. The writer of Hebrews said it best: "These all died in faith" (Heb. 11:13). Dying in faith affirms that Jesus Christ truly is the Messiah.

As we drove away from the home of the fruit gatherer and beautiful vineyard, I said to the pastor, "I will never forget what that man said to me." Truly there is so much to be done, yet so few who really care.

969 Years for What?

Paul said, "Brethren, I count not myself to have apprehended; but this one thing I do, forgetting those things which are behind, and reaching forth unto those things which are before, I press toward the mark for the prize of the high calling of God in Christ Jesus" (Phil. 3:13-14). It has been said, "Few men run well to the end." But, as long as I am able, it is my desire to stay busy for the Lord.

Staying busy is the best thing a Christian can do. In the fifth chapter of Genesis a man named Methuselah is referred to: "All the days of Methuselah were nine hundred sixty and nine years: and he died" (v. 27). We do not have any record in the Bible of anything he ever accomplished or anything he did for man or God. Just think of the food he consumed, the clothes and other necessities he required for 969 years. Yet we have no record of *anything* he ever did!

In contrast, the New Testament in the four Gospels recorded the life of Jesus, who lived only thirty-three years. Let us look at the contrast between Methuselah and Jesus. The Galilean was always about his Father's business in his thirty-three years as he walked this earth. He packed into those thirty-three years more than most would in a thousand years. His accomplishments can never be numbered. Let us never forget that as Christians we have a responsibility and an obligation to God and man.

While traveling in another state, I stopped and asked a man for directions. Among the turns and route numbers, he mentioned an old cemetery I would pass. Upon approaching the cemetery, I stopped my car to stroll through the grounds. One inscription on a tombstone over one hundred and fifty years old read, "A little time on earth he spent, til God for him his angel sent." The dates of birth and death revealed a short life on earth, but I am sure he must have been busy for his Lord. Again, I thought of Jesus, who lived only thirty-three years, but every moment, day and night was packed with activity—either in prayer, in working, in healing the sick, or in helping others.

A verse of Scripture that has always been precious to me is Ephesians 5:16: "Redeeming the time, because the days are evil." It was to the saints at Ephesus, even to the most eminent among them, that Paul addressed that exhortation.

That word *redeeming* is an interesting word. The Greek version here reads "buying up the opportune time" or suggests that we make the best use of our time.

Have you ever thought seriously that in the period of one year there are 8,760 hours? Let us break it down. Generally speaking, 3,000 hours will be spent sleeping. That is the routine eight hours for sleep. Seven hundred hours will be spent eating; 250 hours will be spent in church; 2,200 hours will be spent at work, for eight hours a day, five days a week. That leaves 2,610 hours to do as we please. I ask this question: "We have 2,610 hours to do what we desire. Are we really involved and engaged in the Master's work or just simply playing church? Are we asleep on the job and dragging out feet?" Andrew, as recorded in the Bible, had one talent, that of being a soul-winner; and he used it. He never preached a sermon, never wrote a book, never held an office; but he used what he had to the glory of God.

Down through the ages, when God desires a job to be done, he chooses an individual to do his work. God needs Christians, laymen, businessmen, and people in all other walks of life: the simple "garden variety" Christians to tell others about the living Savior. The reward? Joys untold! The famous John Wesley said, "Give me one hundred men who fear nothing and desire nothing but God. I care not whether they be clergymen or laymen, such alone will shake the gates of hell."

The Bible teaches us to be doers of the word and not hearers only. The call of the disciples was simply, "Follow me." The instructions to the women at the tomb were "Go and tell," and to Jesus' followers after the resurrection, "Go into all the world." His program is every Christian to every creature. It is every Christian's job to be busily engaged in soul-winning. When Paul was free, he won souls. When Paul was in prison, he won souls. When Paul was chained, he won souls. When Jesus was nailed to the cross and dying, he won a soul. The Scripture tells us that he is not willing that any should perish but that all should come to repentance. I am convinced that laymen can reach many, many people with a saving knowledge of the Lord Jesus Christ. None of us will live 969 years as did Methuselah, but I trust we will make every day count for our Lord.

11

More Blessed to Give

In the real estate business one never knows what to expect when he gets a call to come talk with an owner about his property. One day I received a call from a town near Atlanta, to come and discuss the possibility of disposing of the home of an elderly man and woman. It was not the finest house on the street, but it was their castle because they had lived there all their married life.

As we began to discuss the problem, I was told of a foreclosure that was about to take place. They had no money and were living on a small Social Security check. The husband had undergone a very serious operation, which had caused them to borrow on the home to pay the doctors and hospital. Almost a year had passed since they made the loan.

The wife invited me out in the yard to look around, but really she wanted to let me know that her husband was unaware he had only a short time to live. When we went back into the house, I began discussing the Bible with them and found they were very devout Christians among God's chosen saints. I asked the husband about the possibility of raising the money it would take to pay the mortgage and save their home. He informed me that they had no way of raising the money except to sell the home. Those good people had worked hard all their lives, saved, and lived very simply just to make sure they had a place to call home in their old age.

God spoke to me during this conversation; and it seemed as though he put me in their place, experiencing the futility of the situation. The Lord had placed that burden on my heart and clearly made known to me his desire for those Christian people. I wrote them a check without any further questioning. The husband and wife wept with joy. They were speechless for a few moments; then the old gentleman said, "I may never be able to pay you back." "You do not owe me anything. It's a gift." We had a short prayer; and as I drove away they kept waving, arms around each other, crying tears of joy.

I have a letter in my files from those good people. Once in a while, when I feel I am having a tough time, I take the letter out and read what the woman wrote. I thank God that he allowed me to have that blessed experience. Truly it is more blessed to give than to receive. But we should never give expecting a material or monetary return from God. Let us remember that you can give without loving, but you cannot love without giving. "He who takes but never gives may last for years but never lives."

A Rainy-Day Blessing

"But to do good and to communicate forget not: for with such sacrifices God is well pleased" (Heb. 13:16).

One rainy, dreary Monday morning, as I made my way into the Capitol, I met a janitor with his large, four-wheeled canvas cart, emptying the trash that had accumulated overnight. As I approached him, I said, "Good morning; are you happy this morning?" He quickly replied, "No sir, Mr. Legislator, I sho' is not." Hesitantly, I asked if he were ill or if something were troubling him.

"Well, I'm working too hard and not feeling too good," he replied. I reminded him that we all have our problems and then I asked if he were a Christian. "I can assure you, Mr. Legislator, if it wasn't for the Lord, I couldn't make it through the day. Yes sir, I'se a Christian. As a matter of fact, I'se a deacon in the church."

"Well," I said, "Let's talk a minute; I know it's raining outside; it's dreary; it's Monday morning and hard to get started; but have you ever thought about this—Satan will never let you alone. The Bible says, '[He] as a roaring lion walketh about, seeking whom he may devour'" (1 Pet. 5:8).

"You sho' is right, Mr. Legislator, he sho' has been after me just like a lion tearing me apart this morning." I said, "Now, let me remind you of another fact. The world is not your friend. If it is, then you're not God's friend. For he who is the friend of the world is the enemy of God. What, may I ask, would you be doing this morning if you didn't have a job to come to?" "Well," he replied, "I don't know exactly what I'd be doing."

Then I asked, "Did you know the most miserable people in the world are the ones who have nothing to look forward to each morning when they get out of bed?" "Yes, sir," he answered, "that's the truth. But I don't make much money, Mr. Legislator, pushing this cart around these offices and picking up trash."

I am sure that man did not have much of the world's goods, but I reminded him that money does not make a man happy. With conversation and quotes, I tried to give him encouragement and make his day a little happier. Feeling sure he was a Christian, I asked if he had ever read in the Bible that we are to work and make our way by the sweat of the brow. He said, "Yes, sir, I know that." Then I reminded him that the Bible says that a man who does not work and support his household is worse than an infidel.

"Well, sir," he said, "Mr. Legislator, I sho' ain't no infidel, but I do wish the Lord would give me more money." I asked him to think seriously about what would happen if he were to come into a million dollars or just a lot of money that morning. What he would do with it?

He said, "I ain't never had such a thought as that. To tell the truth, I don't know what I'd do with it." Do you reckon you'd handle it wisely?" I asked. "Have you ever thought that you might get in trouble? You might start drinking too much booze or doing things that money would allow you to do that you've never done."

He said, "Well, I've never thought of that." Then I said, "Let's go back to the first thing I asked you this morning, when I said, 'Good morning; are you happy?' and you said, 'No, sir,

I sho' ain't happy.' " Proverbs 16:20 came to my mind and I quoted, "Whoso trusteth in the Lord, happy is he."

"You told me you are trusting in the Lord. The Bible tells us that if we trust in the Lord we are to be happy." He said, "Come to think of it, you is right. I ought to be happy, and I is happy. I just wasn't thinking straight. Mr. Legislator, you has made my day. I'se as happy as a pig in the sunshine." I placed a dollar bill in his hand. We both agreed as we parted that it was good we had met on this dreary morning because it was a blessing to my life, and his day was made happier.

Just a little time, conversation, and encouragement will do wonders if applied with a desire in our hearts to do good and to communicate God's love. The vast majority of people in the world are dying for someone to love them. Show a sincere concern, compassion, and Christlike spirit.

The crying need of the age is for us to faithfully, fearlessly, truthfully hold Jesus up. We are to exalt Christ, not ourselves or our opinions. We are to advocate him, not some man-made doctrine. Kindness and friendship have helped to convert more sinners than arguments, eloquence, or learning.

Let us keep in mind that the middle letter in *pride* is *I,* the middle letter in *sin* is *I,* and the middle letter in *revival* is *I.* The best place to put the *I* is where Paul said in First Corinthians 2:2: "For I determined not to know any thing among you, save Jesus Christ, and him crucified."

The Source of All Joy

The most opportune time for one to present Jesus to an unsaved person is during moments of trouble, sorrow, or weakness; however, God also provides many opportunities for witnessing through joyful moments and by using man's sense of humor. Surely, our Lord must enjoy those numerous encounters when the seed is planted by a humorous twist of events.

To culminate a week's revival, we had planned for the young adult single people and young married couples to meet in the late afternoon, prior to the regular evening service. I was a little late arriving at the church; and, rushing toward the back entrance, I was completely occupied with the theme of the sermon I had prepared on the bride and the bridegroom. As I was about to enter the church, a man breathlessly rushed up to me and demanded, "Where is the bride and bridegroom?" With my thoughts still deeply on my sermon, I spontaneously responded with portions of the Scriptures I planned to use, "Sir, the bridegroom is not here yet; but, praise the Lord, 'the bride says come.' " He asked if I was the preacher and I told him that was correct.

"Well, sir," he said with obvious disgust, "I've been in this business twenty-five years, and you're the first preacher I've met who rejoiced that the bridegroom had not arrived, with the service only minutes away. Now, if you'll excuse me, I must quickly find the bride to photograph her before she sees the groom."

"Hold it!" I said, laughing. "Why didn't you tell me you're a photographer? I didn't even know there was to be a wedding this afternoon!" It took several minutes and the help of a church member to clear up the confusion. The wedding ceremony was at another church close by. Without further delay, he rushed off.

After the conclusion of my service, I found the photographer waiting outside. He said, "Sir, I owe you an apology. I was rushed and spoke rather rudely to you." Pointing out the humor in the misunderstanding, I assured him I had not taken offense to his words and asked if he knew the story about the ten virgins. He was not familiar with it and seemed interested, so I explained how the five wise virgins had prepared to meet the bridegroom, but the five foolish ones waited so late to prepare that they were not ready when the bridegroom came. Afterward they tried to get in, but the door had been closed.

"That's the way it's going to be with all of us one day." I continued, "Jesus is coming for his bride (the church), and many are going to be unprepared. I trust you are ready to meet Christ." He wrote down the Scripture, thanked me, and remarked that our strange and humorous encounter had not only brightened his day, but it had also inspired him to read his Bible.

"And the Spirit and the bride say, Come. And let him that heareth say, Come. And let him that is athirst come. And whosoever will, let him take the water of life freely" (Rev. 22:17).

"Awaken!"

Absurd as this may seem, historians claim that there was a president who slept through his entire administration. March 4, 1849, brought an end to the term of James K. Polk, and at noon Zachary Taylor was to be sworn in as the new president. However, March 4 fell on Sunday, and it was Taylor's desire not to assume official duty on the Lord's Day. So he postponed the official swearing in until Monday.

There was no vice-president at that time; therefore, it became the duty of the president of the Senate, David Rice Atchinson, to serve as interim president. Atchinson had been up late Saturday night; and, upon retiring, he left strict orders not to be disturbed. It is reported that he intermittently dozed or slept throughout Sunday and was not even aware of his official role as acting United States President until after Taylor had been sworn in.

The Bible contains many stories of men's sleeping through events that could have changed, or did change, the course of history. Delilah had Samson's head shaved while he slept in her arms. Jesus asked his disciples to watch while he prayed in the garden of Gethsemane; however, upon his return he found them asleep and said, "Rise up, let us go; lo, he that betrayeth me is at hand" (Mark 14:42). The apostle Paul said, "It is high time to awake out of sleep: for now is our salvation nearer than when we believed. The night is far spent, the day is at hand: let us therefore cast off the works of darkness, and let us put on the armour of light" (Rom. 13:11-12).

There is so much to be done. Let us stay busy witnessing for our Lord, working while it is yet day; for the night cometh when no man can work. Life is full of marvelous possibilities, but the lethargic see them not.

Paul says in the Scriptures, "Wherefore he saith, Awake thou that sleepest, and arise from the dead, and Christ shall give thee light. See then that ye walk circumspectly, not as fools, but as wise" (Eph. 5:14-15).

12
Stepping into Politics

Much prayer and soul-searching was done before I entered into political life as a legislator in the state of Georgia. Christian people—business acquaintances and others from every walk of life—came to me, urging that I seek the office because they felt I could render a service to God and man.

In 1968 I ran for the legislature on Christian principles. My political philosophy has been built on integrity, regardless of possible adverse criticism that might result or the idea, "What's in it for me?" I had much rather vote my convictions and be criticized for doing what is right than to be praised for doing what is wrong. When a political issue is raised, the question in my mind is, "Is it right?" It does not necessarily take a very intelligent man to know right from wrong, but as a Christian in political life, it is essential that we stand up and be counted for what is right. It was Hosea the prophet declaring God's judgment against idolatrous Israel, who gave us the answer: "For the ways of the Lord are right" (Hos. 14:9). A Christian voice in the political roar is a small one on many issues, but I still believe it is just one more candle. We must take action as Christians.

Politics is a vital part of our lives. Some people say all governments are corrupt and that Christian people cannot stay honest in politics. This is far from the truth. Politics does not make people—people make politics. A policy or law cannot be politically right if it is morally wrong. Romans 13:1-3 declares government is ordained of God; therefore those of us involved are ordained of God because we are a part of government. History tells us of people God brought to power for a purpose.

127

When Israel was enslaved in Egypt, God elected Moses and anointed him with wisdom. Esther was made queen to help deliver her people when Haman plotted to destroy the Jews. Her uncle gave assurance that God had raised her up for such a time.

King Solomon prayed to God for an understanding heart and wisdom. In 1 Kings 3:11-12, God said, "Because thou has asked this thing, and hast not asked for thyself long life; . . . and riches, . . . but . . . an understanding to discern judgment. Behold, . . . I have given thee a wise and understanding heart, so that there was none like thee before thee, neither after thee shall any arise like unto thee."

It was Amos who talked about justice for all, Hosea talked about mercy, Isaiah spoke about walking with God; but it was the prophet Micah who put all three of these together and said in Micah 6:8, "He hath shewed thee, O man, what is good; and what doth the Lord require of thee, but to do justly, and to love mercy, and to walk humbly with thy God?"

Speaking to the chief priest and scribes, Jesus said, "Render therefore unto Caesar the things which are Caesar's; and unto God the things that are God's" (Matt. 22:21). For too long we have left the domain of Caesar untouched and forgotten. I am convinced there is no greater place to witness as a Christian than in the political arena. I have come to realize, as never before, that a man who really desires to serve God as a Christian will find open doors, ways, and means to witness to his fellow-man in the political life, that he might never find in other places.

The Bible has much to say about witnessing. Isaiah 43:10 tells us, "Ye are my witnesses, saith the Lord, and my servant whom I have chosen." I feel in my own personal life that God has chosen me as a witness in the Georgia House of Representatives and as a legislator to be an ambassador for Jesus Christ. Paul said, "I am an ambassador in bonds" (Eph. 6:20). An ambassador is one who represents his country and his people to others. So I am an ambassador and witness for my Lord and Savior in the Georgia State House of Representatives.

Many occasions arise when one can speak a word never knowing if the seed falls on fertile soil. One day, several people stepped inside the elevator with me. A man said, "Take me as far up as you can," referring to the top floor. I, too, was going to the top floor and spontaneously said, "Yes, we want to make sure on that last journey we go upward."

When we left the elevator, the man tapped me on the shoulder and said, "Sir, I want to know if one can be sure he's going to heaven when he dies." The Spirit of the Lord gave me the right words: "By your question, I can assume you believe the words in the Bible, so I'll quote you some Scripture and when you get home, read and study them from your Bible. 'These things have I written unto you that believe on the name of the Son of God; that ye may know that ye have eternal life, and that ye may believe on the name of the Son of God'" (1 John 5:13).

He wrote it down and said, "Thank you for giving me these words; I've always wanted something I could hold to that was definite from the Bible, but I've never read that in the Scriptures." We departed, and a seed was planted; a momentary, but a golden opportunity to witness for the Lord Jesus.

It would be almost impossible to exaggerate the seriousness of the present outlook of the political life in our nation today. On a national level or down to a grassroot local level, there is a crisis almost every day. All humanity is involved and heading for eternal destiny; therefore as Christians we need to pray for spiritual awakening among our leaders, that God will intervene: *purge politics . . . purify the church . . . possess people.*

The Bible says, "Behold, I set before you this day a blessing and a curse; A blessing, if ye obey the commandments of the Lord your God, which I command you this day: And a curse, if ye will not obey the commandments of the Lord your God, but turn aside out of the way which I command you this day, to go after other gods, which ye have not known." (Deut. 11:26-28). Never have we had so much to gain by securing divine guidance or so much to lose if we continue our present course.

Daniel Webster made a statement worthy of consideration:

"If we abide by the principles taught in the Bible, our country will grow prosperous, but if we neglect its instructions and authority, no man can tell how sudden a catastrophe may overwhelm us and bury all our glory in profound obscurity."

The first American president, George Washington, gave us some words of wisdom: "It is impossible to govern the world without God. He must be worse than an infidel that lacks faith, and more than wicked that has no gratitude enough to acknowledge."

The only hope for our republic and our survival is to turn toward God. Christians should be in the forefront in making that move, not only in the church of our community but also at the grassroots level, working to the top in Washington, D.C.

Many years ago William Gladstone, the great English statesman and a devout man of God, said, "There is only one international problem. That is to get the gospel of Jesus Christ out to the whole world." One of man's most tragic weaknesses is his failure to learn from history, lessons that for centuries have been recorded by scholars.

It would be good for us to remember the words of the famous historian, Edward Gibbon, who dedicated many years of his life to future generations and to the cause and effects of social changes. In his classic, *The History of the Decline and Fall of the Roman Empire,* he cited five causes for the deterioration of that historic society: (1) the rapid increase of divorce and undermining of the sanctity of the home; (2) the spiraling rise of taxes and extravagant spending; (3) the mounting craze for pleasure; (4) the building of gigantic armaments and the failure to realize that the real enemy lay within the gates of the empire in the moral decay of its people; (5) the decay of religion and fading of faith into a mere form, leaving the people without any guide. Rome makes a rather sobering comparison with our own way of life today in the light of conditions that prevail.

Woodrow Wilson once said, "I would rather fail in a cause that will ultimately succeed than succeed in a cause that will ultimately fail." If we fail, the cause is from within. The permissiveness that is prevalent today is destroying the moral and religious fiber that this country was built upon.

When Benjamin Franklin spoke to the delegates at the Constitutional Convention in Philadelphia, he said, "The longer I live the more I'm convinced that God governs in the affairs of men. If a sparrow cannot fall to the ground without His notice—is it probable that an empire can rise without His aid?—that except the Lord build a house they labor in vain. I firmly believe this; I also believe that without His help we shall succeed no better in this political building than the builders of Babel."

Regretfully, many people are virtually turned off by politics and governments. Some have lost confidence in their government. Let me reassure you, we still have the greatest form of government on earth. God has richly blessed America in spite of all our failures and mistakes. I implore every American to renew his commitments to God and country. Let us keep our country one nation under God and continue to engrave on our coins, "IN GOD WE TRUST."

My prayer in the political life is that we shall rise up to the challenge and turn the tide. This should begin at home and with those of us in public life. You, the people, have elected us to serve, and it is time we tell it like it is, tell the truth, and live the truth. Abraham Lincoln's words should be the motto of every man in political life: "If I go down let me go down linked with truth." I wonder sometimes if those of us in politics are as truthful as we should be.

Everyone may not agree with the political philosophy of the late General de Gaulle of France, but he made a statement worthy of consideration: "Politics is too great an issue to allow it to be left up to just the politicians."

There is danger of power in politics, and if used unwisely, it is a dangerous weapon. Power can corrupt men if they are not right with God. The chaotic conditions of today demand clear minds, levelheaded men with hope and trust in God. Too many people may look to the government as the sole hope and salvation of life. Let me assure you that our hope is not in the United Nations; nor is our hope on Capitol Hill in Wash-

ington, D.C. Our only hope to set right those things that are
wrong in our nation lies with Almighty God. It is not more
legislation that is needed; we have more laws on books today
than we can cope with. The crying need is to put teeth into
our laws and enforce them.

The need is not reformation or turning over a new leaf,
but the need in America is for regeneration. That comes about
only as we become new creatures in Christ Jesus and are born
again. Just imagine what would happen in this great country
of ours if those in political office would let God have his way
in our affairs.

Let us who serve in the political life make sure that we
have the right motives in our hearts as we serve the people.
We are servants of the people, and only when Jesus Christ
lives in one's life can he really come to know and realize his
responsibilities to God and man. We need to seek to know
the mind of God on every issue. My prayer each day as I enter
into the political chamber is, "God help me to guide our ship
of state in the right channel toward the right harbor. Lord,
make plain what I should do; then give me the courage to
do it. Help me to think and to think clearly, to speak when I
need to speak and to speak wisely. Help me to live faithfully,
to do my best always and to leave the results with Thee."

13

Political Concerns

Speech Given to the Georgia General Assembly 1975 Session

Mr. Speaker, ladies, and gentlemen, in the many years I have served in this House, this is the first time I have come to the well of the House on a point of personal privilege; but I feel I must speak out on some things that are on my mind and heart and of a deep conviction and concern.

"First, let me remind you that the seal of this great sovereign state of Georgia, since 1776, reminds us of the land of opportunity. We are known as the Empire State of the South. No other state in these United States of America has more to offer than our beloved state of Georgia. The beautiful mountains, the beaches, the ocean coastline, furnished playgrounds, rivers and streams with their rushing natural beauty, thick forests, deposits of marble and minerals—it is a sportsmen's paradise, with agriculture and industry second to none. These are just a few of the blessings God has bestowed upon us, and we are indeed thankful.

"I would also remind you that Georgia has played a role on the pages of the history of this nation, that will bear testimony that we are of durable stock. Our citizens were present throughout our nation's birth and growth. I submit that as fast as we are moving toward so-called progress, we are departing from fundamentals that are far more vital to our well-being, now, in the future, and for all times, than national wealth and all the things that money can buy. Progress is the American way. It is what makes ours the greatest nation on earth. But let us not forget that democracy can best survive and prosper when its people understand, even more clearly, wherein lies its strength, what it is fighting for, and why. Our forefathers fought and gave their blood for our republic, this great nation, and our form of government.

Some years ago one of our greatest military leaders, General Nathan Twining, while serving as Chief of Staff, said, 'We are holding in our hands the future of our survival: (1) Our Constitution, (2) The Bill of Rights, (3) The Declaration of Independence.' He further stated, 'These are the tools of our defense, our survival.' The point I want to make is this: You and I as legislators have a solemn responsibility. We hold in our hand in a measure the future of this great state, the type of government we want, and the type of government we shall have. Our republic was built on individual freedom, individual opportunity, and individual responsibility. There is a price we must pay to maintain freedom. We must set the example as lawmakers.

"Perhaps one of the greatest men of the century, during the dark days of World War II, said it best as England was burning to the ground from the bombs and devastation of war. Sir Winston Churchill, prime minister of Great Britain, stepped before a microphone and said, 'I have nothing to offer you but blood, tears, toil, and sweat.' He later wrote, 'I felt as if I was walking with destiny and all of my past life had been but a preparation for this hour and for this trial.' Two fingers raised high in the symbol of a V for victory represented faith, courage, dedication, and final victory. Was it worth it? Let me emphatically answer with a positive answer, yes. It meant the difference between survival or surrender.

"By the same token, you and I must put our hands to the plow. We are faced today with the most dangerous time of our civilization. We are a troubled world. The American people are more disturbed and disillusioned than I can ever remember in my lifetime. Our image as political leaders has been damaged, and the confidence of the people has been shaken. The moral and ethical foundation of our political lives is at an all-time low.

"I submit to you that when criminals shoot innocent people down in cold blood and walk the streets free, there is something wrong with our society. When our national debt has reached a staggering figure that is almost beyond our comprehension, of 480 billion dollars, that is equal to 2,262 dollars for every man, woman, and child. The interest alone on that debt is fantastic. Something must be done. Yet with all of our problems, we agree that America is still the greatest nation on earth; and I thank God that I am an American.

"I have studied the lives of many great statesmen involved in politics, and I have come to appreciate Daniel Webster as one of my favorites, for his words of wisdom: 'I was born an American. I will live an American. I shall die an American, and I intend to perform the duties encumbered on me in the character to the end of my career. I mean to do this with absolute disregard of personal consequences. What are the personal consequences? What is the individual man, with all the good or evil that may betide him, in comparison with the good or evil which may befall a great country, and in the midst of great transactions which concern that country's fate? Let the consequences be what they will, I am careless. No man can suffer too much, and no man can fall too soon, if he suffers, or if he fall, in the defense of the liberties and constitutions of his country.' I would like to add my words to the words of Daniel Webster. The Constitution of the United States of America is still working after 200 years because its principles were taken from the Bible.

"The time has come when we need patriots: Democrats and Republicans, labor and management, educated and uneducated, black and white, rich and poor, young and old, to take another look and renew our commitments, participation, and vigilance to make democracy work by carrying the American flag high, to keep step to the music of the Union. The time has come when we in the political life must make clear where we stand and let our people know we need the help of Almighty God as never before.

"Mr. Speaker and fellow colleagues, the question before us

today is, how can we accomplish the tasks? What can I do?
How can I best serve my people back home? It is my firm
belief and conviction that we need to begin moving in the
direction of God. No man can do his best without the help
of Almighty God, whatever his position in life may be. The
Constitution places no requirement upon the government that
it must be hostile to God and religion. I submit that ours is
still a nation under God. This country was founded on Christian
principles. Engraved on our coins are the words, 'IN GOD
WE TRUST.' Our forefathers believed God's divine help and
guidance were necessary for freedom and liberty. Because we
love our country and believe in the American way of life, we
cannot and must not fail God and man.

"Let us never forget that God governs the world. We have
only to do our duty wisely and leave the issues to him. A sound
head, an honest heart, and an humble spirit are the three best
guides through time and eternity. If we acknowledge God in
all our ways, he has promised to safely direct our steps.

"Mr. Speaker, ladies, and gentlemen, I come before this
house to offer a resolution stating that we are willing to humble
ourselves in the sight of Almighty God, asking his divine guidance and his help and praying and seeking wisdom in these
trying days. I invite you to join me by placing your signature
on this resolution, if you so desire, if you feel that with Almighty
God's help we can better solve the problems that face us today.

"I yield the floor, Mr. Speaker, ladies, and gentlemen, with
a prayer in my heart that you share with me some of the con-
cerns for our great state and our country that God has bountifully blessed."

Communism or Christianity?

We are living in a period of conflict between a democratic
and a free way of life, and a totalitarian relationship between
the individual and the state.

What does democracy mean? The dictionary says in part,
"Government by the people in which the supreme power is
vested in the people." It was designed to give everyone an

equal opportunity for life, liberty, and the pursuit of happiness. Democracy, unlike Communism and other heathen governments, is not a dogma, with all the answers coming to us from a dictator or political hierarchy.

Communism has been defined as possessing a language which all people can understand. Its elements are hunger, envy, hate, and death. Karl Marx wrote the bible of Communism, on which Russia's policy is based. He sacrificed health, happiness, and family so that he might devote his life to analyzing the world's ills and prescribe a cure. There is no simple interpretation or clarification of that policy. Sir Winston Churchill once called it "a riddle wrapped up in a mystery inside an enigma."

The survival of democracy does not depend on economic factors alone. A defense for democracy, to be successful, must be built upon faith in God. It must be an unwavering faith with dedication to God as an individual, set forth in God's Holy Word. We must live by God's commandment.

Communism is a false, atheistic, wicked, godforsaken, Satan-inspired religion, with a philosophy:

1. *Total Acceptance of the Cause.* They work toward their goal with tenacious zeal. Perhaps if we would apply the same zeal for our republic and American way of life, we could accomplish more and meet the challenge of the times.

Our forefathers had a cause, a purpose, and a motivating force when they set sail for America. One factor above others was a passion for freedom and democracy. It was the vision, together with economic allurement, that brought more and more people to the new land of opportunity.

They did not have much to live with, but they had something tremendous to live for—freedom to worship God. The life of each one of us is divided into two factors: the things we live with and the things we live for. Nothing enters more deeply into determining the characters of men than the way they handle those two factors. We, the people of America, have more to live with than any other people on earth, thanks to science and prosperity; but when we turn from the things we live with to the things we live for, are we living much better than our forefathers? It is estimated that a hundred years ago the average man had seventy-two wants and sixteen necessities. Today, man has four hundred eighty-four wants and ninety-four necessities, with more than thirty thousand articles and gadgets urged upon him by radio and television advertising; but has all of this made us secure? No, we are a nation of people with a desire for things, and things do not satisfy.

I have framed in my study a one-dollar bill. Many who enter my study want to know the story behind it. It was given to me as expense money for gas on one of my first preaching experiences in a small country church. It is a constant reminder of the time when I started out. I purposed not to ever allow business or money or things of the world to become first place in my life.

Above the dollar bill is the Scripture: "Choose you this day whom ye will serve" (Josh. 24:15). Underneath the dollar bill is this Scripture: "But seek ye first the kingdom of God, and his righteousness: and all these things shall be added unto you" (Matt. 6:33).

Someone once asked one of the richest men in the world, "How much money does it take to make a man happy?" He replied, "Just a little bit more." "A man's life consisteth not in the abundance of the things which he possesseth" (Luke 12:15). True happiness is found only in Christ and Christianity.

The Communist version of the Old and the New Testaments is that both Moses and Jesus were only mythical persons. Khrushchev once said, "God would be banished from the laboratories as well as the schools. Communism has not changed its mind about religion; we remain the atheists that we have always been, and we are doing as much as we can to liberate people that are still under the spell of religion." The Bible says, "He ruleth by his power for ever; his eyes behold the nations: let not the rebellious exalt themselves" (Ps. 66:7).

Christianity is the best armor on earth to fight the evil forces of Communism and all other pagan forces. That means striving toward the absolute standard of honesty, purity, and unselfishness, according to the teachings of Christ.

2. *Total Commitment.* This literally means to surrender all, and it is exactly what the Communists demand and get; but, thank God, we are required to surrender to our Lord and not to man! Only through this commitment can we guard our rights, liberty, freedom, and meet the task of saving our democracy. First, I owe my allegiance to Old Glory, the red, white, and blue; and, if need be, I am willing to sacrifice my life for the freedom and the democracy for which that flag stands.

"For unto us a child is born, unto us a son is given: and the government shall be upon his shoulder: and his name shall be called Wonderful, Counsellor, The mighty God, The everlasting Father, The Prince of Peace" (Isa. 9:6). A total commitment to Jesus Christ will turn the tide for us as a nation.

3. *Total Action.* Recently a Communist from the highest echelon said, "Comrades, it's a magnificent time in which to live!" If only the God-fearing people of the world would exclaim those words with equal fervor: "Christians, it's a magnificent time in which to live." It has been said that when the world is at its worst, the Christians should be at their best. *Now* is the time to take action and to be counted for God. We need an unwavering faith in Almighty God—*a faith that will demand total action.* We need total faith that will cause every American to go into action for God and his country. Elijah was a man who had that kind of faith. He struck fear and trembling into the hearts of men who blasphemed the name and nature of God. Fifty-eight years had passed since the kingdom was divided after Solomon's death. Seven kings had reigned, and each was more wicked than the other; but God is equal to every occasion.

Across the Jordan in Gilead, where people were noted for their rugged character, lived a man named Elijah. He walked alone, calling upon men to forsake their wickedness and return unto the Lord. Elijah was angered by what was going on across the Jordan. He was unpopular, but he was commissioned by God, had total faith in God, and was obedient to God's com-

mand. He had read and knew the recorded promises of God.
Elijah proceeded to put faith into action. He prayed that it
would not rain for three years.

Patiently, step by step, Elijah waited on God and trusted.
The Lord rewarded him, his prayers were answered, and he
carried the keys of heaven for three years. Then he prayed
for rain and the sky was soon black with clouds and a heavy
wind brought a terrific rainstorm.

Christians, the key to preserving our great democracy and
our eternal life is found in these three steps: accept the cause,
commit your life to the cause, and take action for the cause.

Chaplain of the Day

Speaker of the House George L. Smith invited me as a representative to be the chaplain of the day on Thursday, March
8, 1973. Following is the devotion which I gave. The Scripture
is Micah 6:8.

" 'He hath shewed thee, O man, what is good; and what
doth the Lord require of thee, but to do justly, and to love
mercy, and to walk humbly with thy God?'

"Micah was the prophet who foretold the ruin of King Ahab,
the wicked king in the days of Hezekiah. His mission was to
proclaim to Israel and Judah that God's judgment was at hand.
The prophet Micah was God's man for the hour, rebuking and
giving God's warning to the people in that day.

"In that day, as today, God always has a man. When God
desires to shake, shock, or shape any age, he always chooses
a man. Out of the flood waters, God chose a man. From the
bondage of Egypt, God chose a man. On a dusty Damascus
road, God chose a man. A light came from heaven—a man
by the name of Saul fell to the earth, got up and straightway
began to preach Jesus, to become the apostle Paul. Here again
God chose a man. We all have obligations; we are all debtors—
no one is paid up in full. We owe much to many. To win a
game, we are required to keep the rules. To become a lawyer,
doctor, or engineer, one is required to meet specified standards.
One of the most important requirements to become an effec-

tive legislator is integrity. Our freedoms are guaranteed only as we obey certain laws. Our rights are protected only as we fulfill our duties.

"To better understand and to communicate with you my thoughts, let me quote at this point some words of one of the greatest speeches ever made: Daniel Webster's address delivered at the completion of the Bunker Hill Monument on June 17, 1843. Speaking of the coming of the Pilgrim fathers to the new world, he said, 'They brought with them a full portion of the riches of the past in science, art, morals, religion, and literature. *The Bible came with them.* The Bible is a book of faith and a book of doctrine. It teaches man his own responsibility, his own dignity and his equality with his fellow man.'

"In the presence of a professor at Dartmouth College, Mr. Webster laid his hand on a copy of the Scriptures, saying with great emphasis: 'This is the book. I have read through the entire Bible many times. I make it a practice to go through it once a year. It is the book of all others, for lawyers as well as divines, and I pity the man that cannot find in it a rich supply of thought and rule for his conduct. It fits man for life—it prepares him for death.'

"The important question before us is, 'What is required?' I again call your attention to the verse of Scripture from the prophet of God: 'He hath shewed thee, O man, what is good; and what doth the Lord require of thee, but to do justly, and to love mercy, and to walk humbly with thy God.' First of all, let us not forget that God is good. Man is a failure within himself; man is of a depraved nature; God is righteous. No man can be his best without the help of God.

"What is required? 'To do justly.' Webster defines that word as one who is honest, unbiased, fair, right, pure, undefiled, uncorrupted. In other words, to do justly is to observe the laws of God and man. We can sum this up in one word, 'Faith.' The Bible tells us, 'The just shall live by faith' (Rom. 1:17).

"What is required? 'To love mercy,' not just to have mercy. It is one thing to have mercy, something entirely different to love mercy. Let me give a simple example: you lawyers, perhaps, have had an occasion to stand before the judge and court and ask for mercy in behalf of your client. But to love mercy means to show compassion, humility, and concern, and Christ-like kindness, as did Jesus with the woman at the well. That word *mercy* in the Old Testament is the same word, or has the meaning of, *grace* in the New Testament. Grace is defined as unmerited favor or love that Jesus Christ had for a world in sin.

"What is required? 'To walk humbly with thy God.' This one, my friends, is only possible in man's life when he does justly and loves mercy. Walking with God means going God's way. It does not take a very smart man to know which way God is going. Political and professional fame cannot last forever, but conscience void of offense before God and man is an inheritance for eternity.

"Religion, therefore, is a necessary, indispensable element in any great human character. There is no living without it. Religion is the tie that connects man with his Creator. A man without the proper sense of religious duty is without God. Such a man is out of his proper being, out of the circle of all his duties and far away from the purpose of his creation."

14

Going Back Home

How long has it been since you counted the days and hours in anxious anticipation while awaiting the arrival of a loved one? "I'm going home." These words will always be among the sweetest and most heartfelt words on earth. One need not be a seasoned traveler nor endure long separation to experience the inner exultation of going home. Unparalleled joy fills our hearts as we look forward to the open door and outstretched arms of friends and relatives there to greet us and rejoice at our homecoming.

This very moment, there is one who waits for us. The preparations have been made; the days and hours pass swiftly. Loved ones are gathering for the reunion; outstretched arms await us; the door is open. Are you on a road that will lead you to your eternal home, or are you lost on a bypass?

Thirty-five years had passed since I left my childhood home. Then one day I received a call from the pastor of the First Baptist Church located in the vicinity of the hometown of my youth: "Mr. Toles, many of our people in this country remember you as a young man, and I know you have preached many places. We would certainly like to have you come to our church for a week of laymen-led revival. I believe God would use you. Furthermore, don't you think it is about time for you to come back home to preach?"

Immediately I felt an imperative summons from God to accept that invitation. God seemed to say, "You must do this!" We set a date to discuss the possibilities, and agreed to make it a matter of fervent prayer. The pastor, deacons, and I met at the appointed time. After some preliminary discussion of the forthcoming revival, I told them I would be honored to accept their invitation. However they were stunned when I said my acceptance was conditional. I asked, "Brother Pastor and men, how much are you willing to pay? Do you want just another meeting or do you really want a God-sent revival?" For a moment they looked at each other in silence and then in astonishment looked at me. It was evident that they thought I was expecting a guaranteed monetary figure to be placed on the agreement. Their reaction was an answer to prayer. I had asked God to prepare them to pay a great spiritual price, paving the way to a bountiful harvest.

"No, dear brothers, I will not accept a love offering, not as much as a dime. The price I refer to is set down in God's Word. My price to you is a salesman's promise: praying around the clock; first for your life, for me, confessing our sins; and getting our hearts ready. We must be revived before we can expect to show the way to eternal life to others. Gentlemen, for the first time as a layman preacher I'm going to ask that a covenant be made. A covenant is a promise between two parties, which cannot be broken. Are you willing to give wholly of yourselves in every phase of the revival? Will you go out knocking on doors, witnessing at every opportunity? Is the price too high?"

Let me refresh your memory as to the solemnity which God places on a covenant. God established his covenant with Noah and all his descendants forever and set his rainbow in the sky as a token of his covenant to every living creature on earth. It is plain to see that a covenant is not to be taken lightly. Let's search our hearts carefully before committing ourselves to this solemn oath."

The revival fire began to appear. "Mr. Toles, your approach to this is God-inspired; the price of soulwinning is not too high." The covenant was made. We sealed it with prayer, rededicating our lives, asking, "Lord, let it begin in me, right now."

The date for the revival was set. Fervent prayers went up to God, and spiritual preparation in our lives was evident. God revealed to me that he was going to do marvelous things in the lives of many in that community. You who preach understand what I am saying.

In answer to prayer, the church was filled each night, for people came from near and far. One night the pastor announced that that was the largest attendance they had ever had in the church. The entire town was involved: the banker, the doctors, the president of the manufacturing plant, the storekeeper, the druggist, the retired man, the farmer, and the dear old saints of God who had been members of the church fifty or sixty years. My, how they prayed! Everything was done in sweet accord, with the Lord leading. We had a wonderful music program; and since the revival was layman-led, they formed a special all-male choir. Each night I brought a Christian businessman to tell what Jesus Christ meant to him.

For one sermon I chose the subject "The Blackest Sin." I asked these questions. "Who is the greatest sinner, what is the blackest sin, is it murder, is it adultery, is it theft, is it drunkenness, or gambling? 'Is his sin greater than yours?' The greatest and blackest sin is unbelief."

A wonderful thing happened at that service. A man known only to God and me came to the altar when the invitation was given and whispered these words to me: "You mentioned six terrible sins in your sermon. I'm guilty of one, but no one but God knows about this. I cannot go on any longer; I'm miserable and unhappy; I'm guilty. Will you pray with me?" I prayed with him, he confessed his sin to God, and I promised never to reveal his secret. At that moment I realized it was the beginning of a heaven-sent revival. One, paying the price! What a blessing it was!

Three years had passed since we made the covenant with God. I have been back twice since then. The evidence of that first revival still exists. As I have stood in that pulpit I have felt the presence of the Holy Spirit. Each time many have come forward with tear-filled eyes, accepting Jesus into their lives. The covenant made with God continues to reap rewards. I praise God for the privilege of going back to the surroundings of my youth, representing my wonderful Lord Jesus Christ.

There are some who choose not to return home because of broken homes, scars of sin, or bitterness between those once dear. They are fearful of scorn, being turned away, or having to endure the pangs of an aching heart; where there should be joy.

Recently I spoke in a church in a large Southern city, and at the close of the service a very refined, educated lady came to the altar, weeping bitterly. She took my hand and said, "I must talk to you. If your wife is here, would you please have her come sit with us and listen to what I have to say." My wife joined us and the woman raised her sleeves to reveal the scars on both arms, showing the evidence of attempted suicide. She said, "These are marks of sin. Will God forgive me for this? I was unfaithful to my husband; he left me, and I'm a wretched miserable soul, lost and alone." Through Scripture and prayer she found the healing balm of our merciful and forgiving Lord. The path to her release from sin was awash with bitter tears, but not impossible. Another earthly sin was laid at the foot of the cross.

The layman-led revival is something that will always be in my memory. It began with a few dedicated Christian men. The spirit of revival overflowed through the church, reaching into the homes. The reaping of the harvest continues onward with God's blessings, and without bounds. "Faith, if it hath not works is dead" (Jas. 2:17), says the Bible.

Home on this earth may not always measure up to our desires, hopes, and ambitions. Yet, for most, we leave it with heavy hearts, a wave of the hand, and reassuring words, "See you soon." From time-to-time, we reach out briefly to recapture the treasured moments of the past, to enter the open door; but time can never be more than a dream or a memory. With tears in our eyes, we look upon the shuttered house and listen, only to hear the echoes of our loved ones' voices. Each of us will reach the moment in our lives when there are no more homecomings of our youth. They are replaced with sweet, aching memories.

God has promised us a homecoming—a reunion celebration

to join him with every loved one who has accepted his invitation. God sent his Son, a personal messenger, to you, to give that invitation. He has promised unending joy. Have you accepted? Accept and share the good news. Look forward to the reunion in our heavenly home.

It is so simple to make your decision known to him: "Lord, I accept you as my personal Savior; I want to be part of your reunion. In my heart I want to feel the inner exultation of knowing that someday "I'm going home!"

15

Which Road Now?

Where are we headed? No one has the answer. Not long ago, I read, "The purpose of the road does not serve as a platform or a stationary waiting, but to lead to some destination." By the same token, we are on the road of life, traveling to our final destination. We, as individuals, are on our way to heaven or hell. Life is a journey. Some of us arrive at our destinations sooner than others. Where *are* we headed?

The Bible teaches that Jesus is coming again. "Therefore be ye also ready: for in such an hour as ye think not the Son of man cometh" (Matt. 24:44). His coming is *imminent*. That means he could appear at any moment. Because the coming of Christ is imminent, we are exhorted to be in a constant expectancy, waiting for his return. Everything moves toward the second coming of our Lord Jesus Christ. (Note Matt. 24:32-42.) The coming of the Lord Jesus will be as unexpected as the coming of the flood in the day of Noah. Never forget that Jesus said, "I will come again" (John 14:3).

From time to time, I visit the cemetery where many of my loved ones are buried. I stand with praise and thanks to God for the realization that this is not the end but just the beginning. Jesus said, "Because I live, ye shall live also" (John 14:19). "I am the resurrection, and the life" (John 11:25).

Paul's words to the Corinthians became a new hope and revelation. Each time I stand at a grave, I ponder on his words as recorded in 1 Corinthians 15: "But if there be no resurrection of the dead, then is Christ not risen. And if Christ be not risen, then is our preaching vain, and your faith is also vain" (vv. 13-14). Thank God for the Bible that teaches the fact of the "empty tomb," for God's Word is true; it is our only hope, for our faith is in a risen Savior. Imagine an eternity with Christ the Lord: no more sorrow, tears, or heartache! God shall wipe away all tears.

A good question to ask is, "Where are we today in God's timetable of history?" Perhaps the following story will illustrate the answer to that question. There was an old gentleman whose education had not gone beyond the third grade. He and his wife had one cherished piece of furniture, a grandfather clock that had been handed down from generations past. Many nights, he would awake and listen for the strike of the clock to know the time. One night, something went wrong with the old clock's mechanism; and instead of stopping at twelve, the midnight hour, the clock struck twelve, thirteen, fourteen, and fifteen times. In his astonishment and fright, he shook his wife and said, "My, My, wake up! wake up! I never knowed it to be so late." His grammar was not correct, but his concept of time was worthy of consideration. *It is later than we think!*

Deuteronomy 8:11 says, "Beware, that thou forget not the Lord thy God, in not keeping his commandments, and his judgments, and his statutes, which I command thee this day." "And it shall be, if thou do at all forget the Lord thy God, and walk after other gods, and serve them, and worship them, I testify against you this day that ye shall surely perish. As the nations which the Lord destroyeth before your face, so shall ye perish; because ye would not be obedient unto the voice of the Lord your God" (Deut. 8:19-20).

Do not blame God for world conditions. God gives strength for every burden, courage for every battle, light for the night, and pardon for sins. Many have turned their backs and forgotten God. We are living in a day when we are guilty of dethroning God and deifying man. God is here, God is there, God is everywhere, and God is alive and lives forevermore! He has granted to his most treasured creation, 'human beings,' the right and privilege to seek his will, to do his will, and to follow his directions and commandments.

The history of Israel is an example of a nation that God loved and chose. They were blessed above all the nations of the earth, but they rejected him time after time. When we study the Old Testament, we marvel at God's patience. Years passed and finally God said, "That's enough!" God's wrath was kindled, and he allowed a heathen, barbarous nation to judge his people. In Ezekiel 22:30, we read, "And I sought for a man among them, that should make up the hedge, and stand in the gap before me for the land, that I should not destroy it: but I found none." The nation of the Jews was in desperate condition in that day. Their defenses were down. God looked for someone to fill the gap and save the nation, but none was found.

"Gap" is an interesting word. Webster defines it as being a break or opening, as in a fence or a wall. As a young boy on the farm, I remember one morning before daylight that there was a rap on the back door. One of the tenants had come to awaken my father and tell him that all the cows were out of the pasture and were in a neighbor's cornfield. Quickly, my father and I arose, got the hammer and staples, drove the cows back into pasture, and then repaired the gap in the pasture fence. There needs to be fence mending among our people today. There is a gap in some of our lives. We have left the gate open to Satan. The fence is down, and the devil has slipped in. We are out "grazing" in the world, out of tune and out of touch with God.

As we turn to the New Testament and read the twenty-third chapter of Luke, we find Jesus brought before Pilate. They began to accuse him, saying, "We found this fellow perverting the nation, and forbidding to give tribute to Caesar, saying that he himself is Christ a King" (v. 2). As we read on, we find that Pilate says, "I find no fault in this man" (v. 4). That infuriated the people; and in the fifth verse we read, "He stirreth up the people, teaching throughout all Jewry, beginning from Galilee to this place." In other words, the only fault they could find with Jesus was that he "stirred up" the people. Not since the Nazarene walked this earth 2,000 years ago has there been a greater need for a "stirring" of people to God as there is today. If Jesus were alive today, some would label him "the great disturber." As individuals and as a nation, we need our hearts stirred and warmed, causing us to turn to God before it is too late.

Traveling across America as a layman speaking to people of all denominations, I am convinced that we need more preaching on repentance. That word *repentance* means a change of heart and a change of mind. Our world is rushing toward a catastrophe. I see coming chaos, as surely as the shepherds saw the star of Bethlehem. I am no prophet; neither am I an alarmist. I am a realist. All signs of this present hour point to one of two things: either an increasing apostasy and falling away to the utter breakdown of civilization, or a spiritual awakening and turning to God. I pray it will be the latter.

In our nation's capital, the Washington Monument dominates the skyline of the city standing some 555 feet tall. Inside the beautiful monument, set within the walls, are 190 carved tribute blocks. Among the expressions of the faith of the people are Bible phrases that include Proverbs 10:7: "The memory of the just is blessed"; John 5:39: "Search the scriptures"; Exodus 28:36: "HOLINESS TO THE LORD."

Yes, truly God is in the history of this nation. We Christians are pilgrims and strangers. The journey is long and laborious; there are many miry places, with pollution and corruption in every direction. Satan is on the move, with spiritual wickedness in high places; but our God is still on the throne and able to deliver us. God is mightier than the devil and all of his angels.

Again, the question, "Where are we headed?" Looking over my many years of lay preaching, political, and business life, I am convinced that the answer cannot be found in man. Mankind has been searching for peace, justice, and equality for thousands of years. We have prophecies in Isaiah of the second coming of Christ to establish his kingdom and rule the world. "And it shall come to pass in the last days, that the mountain of the Lord's house shall be established in the top of the mountains, and shall be exalted above the hills; and all nations shall flow unto it. And many people shall go and say, Come ye, and let us go up to the mountain of the Lord, to the house of God of Jacob; and he will teach us of his ways. And we will walk in his paths; for out of Zion shall go forth the law, and the word of the Lord from Jerusalem. And he shall judge among the nations, and shall rebuke many people; and they shall beat their swords into plowshares, and their spears into pruninghooks: nation shall not lift up sword against nation, neither shall they learn war any more" (Isa. 2:2-4).

The most important of all questions is not about where we are headed but, "What is our destination?" The Bible tells us to prepare to meet God. Let me urge you who are lost. Jesus Christ in plain words gave the plan of salvation: "Verily, verily, I say unto you. He that heareth my Word, and believeth on him that sent me, hath everlasting life, and shall not come into condemnation; but is passed from death unto life" (John 5:24).

One of the most frequent questions that has come to me through the years is, "What can I do?" First, let us hear the loving voice of the Savior as he cried to each of us, "Come unto me." Many times when I preach, I am well aware that there are more words of truth and wisdom in the Bible to govern the affairs of men than all the law books in the entire fifty states of America, if only men would look to God's Word and obey his laws and commandments. That seems to be the hardest task of all.

It is said that when Irving Berlin wrote the song "God Bless America," in 1917, it got nowhere. As a matter of fact, it was almost a flop. During the dark days of World War II, a lovely lady with a beautiful voice, known as "Undisputed first lady of radio," Kate Smith, dusted off the old tune, stepped before the microphone, and sang the song. It soon became the number one hit in America. People all across this country began to sing "God Bless America" from their hearts. I wonder if we, as Americans, should not dust off the sin in our lives, come clean with God as individuals, and ask God to once again bless America.

Which way can we move to get out of this dilemma we now face as a nation religiously, politically, and economically?

It seems that our nation is coming apart at the seams.

In my lifetime, we have come from horse and buggy days to man's first walk in space. Science, technology, and medical advances are almost unbelievable. Our accomplishments are great; we have learned to fly like a bird, go to the moon, and swim on the bottom of the ocean like a fish; but we have not yet learned how to live on God's earth.

During one of my last conversations with my father as he lay stricken on his deathbed, we discussed the farms, tenants, taxes, and conditions during his lifetime. The conversation turned to the spiritual life and blessings of God, and the senselessness of worry and fretting the future as a Christian. He said something that I shall never forget: "Son, remember you've got to live a lifetime to learn how to live." In other words, when it is time to leave this world and go directly to our heavenly home, we are just beginning to have enough wisdom to realize what life is all about.

Since the beginning of time, men have searched for ways to control their destiny, the destiny of nations, and the destiny of the world. Each generation marvels at the achievements of the past and dreams of unraveling the mysteries that remain, confident that their contribution will provide a master key to solving the ills of the world. At best, discoveries, theories, and philosophies are temporary answers and relief for the world.

Medical scientists have found prevention and cures for innumerable dreaded, crippling, or fatal diseases. Yet, they cannot compete with the rapid pace with which mankind devises new ways to defile the human body. Scientists and technologists have split the atom and put man into space, proclaiming that their achievements will benefit all mankind. Yet, they cannot provide the rudiments of safeguards against the exploitation of their awesome discoveries.

Politicians swear by the words and platforms of their party and leaders; yet they are perplexed and disturbed when these ideas become realities and fail to fulfill the needs of the people.

The combined efforts of the United Nations can do no more than divert and postpone aggressive actions motivated by nations desperately seeking solutions.

Economists are grasping and pleading for an answer that will relieve the anxiety of the growing number of people striving to provide the simple necessities of life. Educators are having to cope with an educational system that is delusive in light of the realities of life. No longer are the young assimilating instruction and accepting it as being synonymous with truth. Labor has never been more acutely aware of the devastating affects of an unbalanced supply and demand. Control is not only out of reach but also growing more distant. Lawmen, judges and social workers are appalled by the growing number of crimes and their heinous natures. Learned men have long theories about methods of prevention and correction. Their theories fall short, and so we continue to rely on incarceration.

Even the farmer, with his modern machinery and scientific agricultural know-how, diligently searches for a way to stay in harmony with nature. Each year, with perseverance and tenacity but without assurance, he strives for a harvest that will help feed a hungry world. Theologians throughout the world know not what tomorrow brings, but they do know God is in command.

No, my friend, I do not have the answers to where we are headed as a nation, but rest assured, we all have an eternity waiting in our future. The decision where that eternity will be spent must be made while we have life and an opportunity to choose our destination. The united efforts of mankind throughout all time could not provide the Utopia man desires; however, it is God's will that man will continue to seek ways that will serve and benefit all people.

No man has all the answers, but it is my sincere belief that God has given us his instructions and his promise that will never fail if we as a nation and as individuals will take heed to the words recorded in the Bible, which I submit for your prayerful consideration: "If my people, which are called by

my name, shall humble themselves, and pray, and seek my
face, and turn from their wicked ways; then will I hear from
heaven, and will forgive their sin, and will heal their land"
(2 Chron. 7:14).

God alone has the total answer for a disillusioned world.
His answer starts with giving mankind a choice. Each individual
must decide to accept or reject his plan.

Epilogue

In reverence I stand in a pulpit surveying the people who have come to hear God's Word and momentarily I experience astonishment as I think how close I came to missing his will for my life.

Look with me from the platform: every seat taken, the aisles filled with chairs. The organ and piano are playing, "The King Is Coming." My eyes are clouded with tears as others are wiping away tears. Silently I pray, "O God, how close I came to missing this, experiencing the presence of the Holy Spirit." God clearly replies, "This was my way and my will for you."

Through these many years I have learned so much about God's wonderful grace, his love, and his enduring patience. For the concern and love God has given me for others, I am thankful. I rejoice with the angels for those who have accepted Jesus into their lives. I praise him now for all the afflictions, all the hardships he allowed to happen to me until I accepted his will for my life.

To tell others about Jesus is the greatest business on earth, the rewards are immeasurable, and the retirement plan is out of this world and for eternity.

"I am crucified with Christ: nevertheless I live; yet not I, but Christ liveth in me: and the life which I now live in the flesh I live by the faith of the Son of God, who loved me, and gave himself for me" (Gal. 2:20).

The greatest ambition of one who knows he is crucified with Christ is to serve him; he is jealous of nothing; his fight is sin and Satan. He is dead in Christ.

With the psalmist I say, "It is good for me that I have been afflicted; that I might learn thy statutes" (Ps. 119:71). Oh, what a Savior! Yes, I truly learned Jesus Christ comes to where you are to take you to where you ought to be.